They Called Him Buckskin Frank

They Called Him Buckskin Frank

The Life and Adventures of Nashville Franklyn Leslie

Jack DeMattos
and
Chuck Parsons

with a Foreword by John Boessenecker

Number 19 in the A.C. Greene Series

UNT PRESS

Denton, Texas

Printed in the United States of America.
10 9 8 7 6 5 4 3 2 1

Permissions:
University of North Texas Press
1155 Union Circle #311336
Denton, TX 76203-5017

The paper used in this book meets the minimum requirements of the American National Standard for Permanence of Paper for Printed Library Materials, z39.48.1984. Binding materials have been chosen for durability.

Library of Congress Cataloging-in-Publication Data
Names: DeMattos, Jack, 1944- author. | Parsons, Chuck, author.
Title: They called him Buckskin Frank : the life and adventures of Nashville Franklyn Leslie / by Jack DeMattos and Chuck Parsons.
Other titles: A.C. Greene series ; no. 19.
Description: Denton, Texas : University of North Texas Press, [2018] | Series: Number 19 in the A.C. Greene series | Includes bibliographical references and index.
Identifiers: LCCN 2018004890| ISBN 9781574417128 (cloth : alk. paper) | ISBN 9781574417203 (ebook)
Subjects: LCSH: Leslie, Frank, 1842- | Outlaws--Arizona--Tombstone--Biography. | Tombstone (Ariz.)--Biography.
Classification: LCC F819.T6 D46 2018 | DDC 979.1/053092 [B] --dc23
LC record available at https://lccn.loc.gov/2018004890

They Called Him Buckskin Frank: The Life and Adventures of Nashville Franklyn Leslie is Number 19 in the A.C. Greene Series

The electronic edition of this book was made possible by the support of the Vick Family Foundation.

This biography is dedicated to the memory of
Joseph G. Rosa
November 20, 1932 – January 17, 2015

Table of Contents

List of Illustrations

FOREWORD

Buckskin Frank Leslie was one of the most notable characters of the Old West. During the 1880s he cut a wide swath in Arizona Territory. Leslie achieved fame for riding with Wyatt Earp as a participant in pursuit of the notorious gang known as the Cowboys, and later for killing one of their number, Billy Claiborne, in a stand-up shootout in Tombstone. Young Claiborne had managed to survive the so-called Gunfight at the O.K. Corral, but he could not survive the deadly six-gun of Buckskin Frank. Leslie achieved notoriety in 1889 when he shot and killed his paramour, Mollie Edwards, for which he was sent to the territorial prison at Yuma. In between he saw both adventure and drudgery as a gunfighter, gambler, Army scout, saloon keeper, and rancher.

Frank Leslie was a product of the frontier. During the nineteenth century, America had a profound gender imbalance, with females in the minority. Young, single, unpropertied males were a surplus; they were unneeded. As a result they tended to drift to the frontier regions. There was nothing to keep them at home: no prospects for a good job, for a wife, for a family. Many were impoverished and poorly educated. But what they lacked in marketable skills they made up for in reckless courage and thirst for adventure. Many drifted from one frontier to another—from California to Idaho to Nevada to Arizona—always hoping to strike it rich in gold, silver, cattle, or business. Buckskin Frank Leslie was such a man, a true frontiersman, whose colorful career and violent life are not forgotten.

Violence was a hallmark of all frontier communities. Numerous studies have shown that the frontier regions of the American West were extremely violent, and Southern Arizona, where Buckskin Frank made his mark, was no exception. Pima County, one of the four original counties in Arizona, in 1880 was one of the largest in the U.S., consisting of most of the current counties of Pima, Cochise, Graham, Santa Cruz, and Greenlee. It encompassed 300 miles from New Mexico east to Yuma County, and from the Mexican border 150 miles north to the Gila River. Its 23,000 square miles were almost the same size as the state of West Virginia. The silver mining town of Tombstone was settled in 1878 and soon afterward such mining camps as Charleston, Contention City, and Bisbee sprang up. By 1880 Pima County's population had boomed to 20,000, with about 7,000 people living in Tucson, the county seat.

Arizona was a huge region of deserts and mountains, populated with scattered mining camps, settlements, and ranches. It was so remote that it attracted hundreds of fugitives, robbers, and desperadoes. Pima County was then one of the most violent regions in the United States. Between October 1879 and October 1880 the county had twenty-five murders. When adjusted for population, this equals a rate of 125 homicides per 100,000, which is twenty-two times higher than the modern national murder rate. In 1881, Pima County, which by that time no longer included what are now Cochise and Graham Counties, with a population of about 17,500, saw at least eight homicides, for a rate of 45 per 100,000. In 1882 there were at least eighteen murders, with a resulting rate of 103 per 100,000. When deaths from Apache warfare are included, the county's homicide rates were even higher. By comparison, in 2008 Tucson had a murder rate of 14 per 100,000, which was considered very high and made newspaper headlines.

Much of the violence was caused by competition for gold, silver, lead, cattle, and women. People of that era believed that social problems and personal difficulties were not things to be solved by government. Men were expected to "kill their own snakes," to resolve their own difficulties. Police and sheriffs were few and far between. At the same time many men on the frontier were young, far from the settling influences of the mothers and sisters whom they had left back at home. They were imbued with reckless courage, too much cheap liquor, and an abundance of Colt revolvers and Winchester rifles. It was a deadly brew, and helps explain Frank Leslie's violent life.

This biography is the result of exhaustive research by two of the most knowledgeable historians of western outlaws and lawmen. Jack DeMattos has studied the topic since the late 1950s, and is the author of seven books and countless magazine articles about the Old West. Chuck Parsons has written fifteen books and dozens of articles on frontier justice. In these pages they put forth a rip-roaring tale of the tumultuous life and mysterious death of Buckskin Frank Leslie.

John Boessenecker

Acknowledgments

First and foremost, the authors must acknowledge the many contributions that William A. "Billy" Mills of Perry, GA, has made to this biography. Although a seasoned researcher, Billy has only recently turned his attention to Wild West history. He took the time from a project of his own to assist the authors with their Buckskin Frank Leslie research. In addition to finding significant new Leslie material on his own, he also pointed the authors in the direction where additional documentation could be uncovered.

The authors also want to thank Cathie S. Grant of British Columbia, Canada. She is the great-granddaughter of Leslie's last wife, Nora Cast Leslie. Cathie generously provided much-needed information concerning her great-grandmother's life with Buckskin Frank.

David E. Dean III of Dundee, New York, is the great-grandson of Leslie's long-time associate John Ralph Dean. David and his wife Jane have many of the personal effects that once belonged to John Ralph Dean—including a previously unpublished photo of Leslie as he appeared toward the end of his long life. The authors wish to thank David and Jane Dean for granting the authors permission to reproduce this photo in our biography.

The authors also gratefully acknowledge the following friends involved in Wild West history, whose trails have often crossed our own:

Bob Boze Bell, Cave Creek, AZ

John Boessenecker, San Francisco, CA

Robert K. DeArment, Sylvania, OH

Charles David Grear, New Braunfels, TX

Dave Johnson, Zionsville, IN

Robert G. McCubbin, Santa Fe, NM

Leon C. Metz, El Paso, TX

Rick Miller, Harker Heights, TX

James A. Mundie, Kenner, LA

Bob Palmquist, Tucson, AZ

Chris Penn, Marsham, England

Gary L. Roberts, Tifton, GA

Meghan Saar, Lumberton, TX

William B. Secrest, Fresno, CA

Tom Todd, Show Low, AZ

Roy B. Young, Apache, OK

Finally, the authors want to acknowledge the longtime support of our wives, Pat Parsons and the late Sandi DeMattos. Over the years these ladies have supported our efforts to research the history of the Wild West when it was populated with colorful characters such as the man they called "Buckskin Frank."

Prologue

"Buckskin Frank" Leslie felt comfortable in the Oriental Saloon, one of the best in Tombstone, Arizona Territory. He tended to keep to himself, rarely even arguing with anyone. Tending bar and speaking with thirsty customers and generally minding his own business was what Leslie did best. He avoided drinking while on duty, but did occasionally enjoy a good cigar.

Now, a little after 7:00 a.m., Leslie was on duty, gabbing with some friends. In strode a young man called Billy. He was William Floyd Claiborne his full name, angry at something or someone, already carrying too much liquor. His language was insulting, filled with oaths, offensive enough that Leslie, as the head bartender on duty, felt compelled to demand Claiborne leave the premises. Claiborne was sober enough that he did leave.

But then he returned, and the pushing and insulting and foul language continued. Leslie had had enough and this time he forcefully led the young drunk out. Leslie was fully aware of the potential danger of what an angry young man with too much liquor in him wearing a weapon could cause. Claiborne threatened: "That's all right, Leslie. I'll get even on you." Having gotten Claiborne outside Leslie returned to his companions.

Only moments later however another man entered, greatly concerned. "Claiborne's outside, with a rifle. He says he's going to shoot you."

Leslie was annoyed by this action of a drunken man who had no reason to threaten him. But it could not be ignored. The bartender now placed his newly lit cigar on the edge of the bar and thought how to deal with the threats. It was best to face his opponent; he knew he had the advantage of being sober and deliberate, whereas Claiborne was drunk. Out on the sidewalk he noticed the end of a rifle barrel sticking out behind a fruit stand. He knew it was Billy Claiborne.

"Billy, don't shoot. I don't want you to kill me, and I don't want to have to shoot you."

The words had no effect. Billy Claiborne raised the rifle, aimed at Leslie and fired. He missed. Leslie then acted the only way he knew how. He leveled his pistol and fired once, aiming for the breast. After the first shot he cocked the pistol again . . . ready for a clumsy agonizing reaction from the mortally wounded Claiborne.

As Leslie advanced Billy had scarcely the strength to utter a few words: "Don't shoot again. I am killed."

As the sound of the gunshot echoed away and the smoke cleared a policeman approached. Leslie handed him the pistol. He then spoke to the lawman, relating that he was sorry for what he had done, adding: "I might have done more, but I couldn't do less."

Now on the fourteenth day of November, 1882, Frank Leslie returned to the bar, on duty again. He picked up the cigar. It was still smoking.

***

They called him Buckskin Frank. He called himself Nashville Franklyn Leslie—which might (or might not) have been the name he was born with. While he never achieved the national fame as did Wyatt Earp, both Earp and Leslie are remembered as gunfighters—and the gunfights that both are best remembered for happened in Tombstone, Arizona

Territory. Leslie managed to remain a neutral figure during the volatile Wyatt Earp era, during which Earp and Leslie seemed content to stay out of each other's way.

The two men couldn't have been more different. As a six-footer, Earp was considered tall for that day and age. Leslie measured only 5-feet, 7-inches (in boots) but was every bit of Earp's equal as a gunman. Earp was a career lawman and gambler. Leslie was neither—although he did, on occasion, ride with a posse and pin on a deputy's badge for very short periods. No evidence has been found showing that Leslie was a professional gambler, or sporting man, in the sense that Wyatt Earp, Bat Masterson, and Luke Short were.

Wyatt Earp's time in Tombstone, event-filled as it may have been, was all over by the spring of 1882. Buckskin Frank's time in Tombstone, as well as other parts of Arizona and Mexico, spanned the entire decade of the 1880s. During that decade, Leslie played on a much larger stage, for a much longer time, than Wyatt Earp had. Leslie's Arizona years included nearly every aspect of mining and ranch life that Earp was not part of. If there was one constant in Leslie's life in Arizona and elsewhere, it was his mining activities. Leslie was involved in mining projects throughout much of his adult life, during which he located numerous copper and silver mining claims.

As a cattleman, Leslie was a partner in one of the largest ranches in southeastern Arizona. Between his mining and ranching activities he found time to serve as a scout, and courier, during the Apache campaigns, and patrol the border as a Mounted Customs Inspector. When in Tombstone, Leslie usually could be found working behind the bar of a saloon. During his early Tombstone years, Leslie was actually a partner in two saloons at the same time.

Despite having a far more colorful life than other celebrated Wild West figures, Leslie failed to attract the attention of a biographer until well into the twentieth century. It wasn't until 1962 that the first attempt of a biographer appeared in the form of a sixty-four-page pamphlet called

Silver, Sex and Six-Guns: Tombstone Saga of Buckskin Frank Leslie by Douglas D. Martin. This was closely followed by Colin Rickards's 1964 effort entitled *Buckskin Frank Leslie: Gunman of Tombstone*, which was a hardcover volume, but contained only forty-five pages and had a limited run of only 450 copies. The third, and most extensive, effort appeared in 1999. It was written by Don Chaput and was simply titled *"Buckskin Frank" Leslie*. It was a soft-cover volume containing 143 pages with a limited press run of 750 copies. The most recent volume devoted to Leslie was Ben T. Traywick's *Tombstone's "Buckskin Frank": Nashville Franklyn Leslie*, which was published in 2013 and contained a total of 189 pages, of which eighty-one were devoted to illustrations.

No attempt will be made here to critique those four earlier biographies of Leslie. Each of them contributed something to our knowledge of Leslie's life. This biography acknowledges the contributions of those earlier works, and will expand upon the information they contained. Further, this biography will offer new information on Leslie's life and death that has not appeared previously. Leslie's story will be presented using documents that appeared when the events actually happened. Whenever possible, these events will be told in Leslie's own words.

Nashville Franklyn Leslie has never been the recipient of the Hollywood glorification accorded Wyatt Earp, resulting in numerous motion pictures and a television series. There was a time, during the 1880s, when Earp and Leslie were equals as far as notoriety was concerned. During that tumultuous decade nearly everyone in Arizona, citizen and soldier alike, knew Leslie's name. They knew him as a man who was a key player—and not a peripheral figure—in the actual history of Pima and Cochise County, Arizona. They all knew of his exploits, good and bad. They usually called him by the moniker that was his alone and would immediately identify him in that time and place.

They called him Buckskin Frank.

They Called Him Buckskin Frank

Chapter 1

The Birth of Buckskin Frank Leslie

"I, Nashville Franklyn Leslie, was born near San Antonio, Texas on the 18th day of March 1842 and am now a resident of Tombstone, Arizona and have been a resident of Arizona for nine years." The man we remember as "Buckskin Frank" Leslie wrote these words on an application for employment to Collector of Customs Joseph Magoffin on March 10, 1886. Leslie was hired as a mounted inspector, responsible for patrolling part of the border between Arizona and Mexico. The words that Leslie penned on his job application are the earliest known in which he recorded his date and place of birth.[1]

Supporting evidence for March 18, 1842, being the correct birth date was given by the Sunday, March 27, 1881, edition of the *Arizona Weekly Citizen,* which reported "Frank Leslie, the well known scout who was with General Custer, celebrated his thirty-ninth birthday last Friday." This item was a reprint from a Tombstone paper of the previous week. The "last Friday" in question was actually Friday, March 18, 1881, which was indeed Leslie's thirty-ninth birthday.[2]

Leslie claimed to be "born near San Antonio," and future research may validate his claim. The three United States Federal Census records that have been found for Leslie (1880, 1910, and 1920) all give his birthplace as Texas. So saying, it must be noted that an 1889 newspaper account asserted that Galveston, Texas (located some 247 driving miles from San Antonio) was Leslie's actual birthplace.[3]

In the 1886 Great Register for Cochise County A.T., Leslie was recorded as Voter No. 1204 as "Nashville Franklin [*sic*] Leslie, age 44." His birthplace was given as the "Texas Republic" and contained the further information that he had been "Naturalized by Annex of Texas to U.S." Thus, Leslie had actually been born in a foreign country in 1842, since the Republic of Texas was an independent nation between its founding on March 2, 1836, and its annexation to the United States on December 29, 1845. Undoubtedly the thousands of people who were born in Texas during that period, including Leslie, automatically became U.S. citizens, following the annexation, without formal paperwork being required. In any case, the words "naturalized by Tex to U.S." provides strong evidence that Texas was indeed Leslie's actual birthplace.[4]

There was another person named Leslie who lived in a town "near San Antonio," who was possibly a relative of Nashville Franklyn Leslie. That person was Andrew Jackson "Jack" Leslie, a first cousin once removed of President Andrew Jackson. He was born in Humphreys County, Tennessee, in 1814, arrived in Texas during 1835, and took part in early battles against Santa Anna's soldiers. The Republic of Texas awarded him 640 acres of land for his service, once Santa Anna's forces had been defeated. The land was located in Helotes, Texas, on the far northwest side of San Antonio. On January 29, 1852, Texas conducted Survey No. 217, which described Jack Leslie's land as being at the intersection of Leslie Road and Culebra Road in Helotes, Texas.

Jack Leslie also enlisted for a month's service as a Texas Ranger on October 12, 1855. He appears to have remained a bachelor, since no records are known to exist showing that he married or had children. The seriously ill Andrew Jackson "Jack" Leslie signed his will on November 10, 1884, stating that "I bequeath all of my worldly goods of whatever kind to my beloved grand-nephew G.G. Leslie." He died on February 5, 1885.[5]

While the authors cannot state with certainty that Andrew Jackson "Jack" Leslie and Nashville Franklyn "Buckskin Frank" Leslie were related to each other, we are certain that Jack Leslie was exactly the type of person that Frank Leslie would have been proud to claim as a relative. There were also at least four other individuals named Leslie living "near San Antonio" around the time of Nashville Franklyn Leslie's birth. They were listed on Bexar County, Texas, Tax Rolls as follows: J.A. Leslie in 1841, John R. Leslie in 1841 and 1842, J.W. Leslie in 1840, and J.J. Leslie in 1842.[6]

The many articles and the four books written about Frank Leslie have often portrayed him as being a Wild West version of Baron Munchausen. Some of the wildest stories date back to the late nineteenth century—including an account from 1893, by a San Francisco reporter who claimed "the story of his life is a romance. Born in Virginia in 1842 of a good family he went to Heidelberg to study medicine, his brother at the same time going to West Point for a military education. When the Civil War broke out in 1861 Frank returned to his old home in Virginia and entered the Confederate army as a bugler, while his brother joined the Union forces."[7]

Leslie probably never set foot in Virginia, and he certainly wasn't born there. Only on two occasions would he make the deceptive claim of a Virginia birth, first to the San Francisco reporter in 1893 then on a wedding certificate in 1896. On all of the other documents that exist for him—before 1893 and after 1896—Leslie consistently gave Texas as his birthplace. Nothing has turned up showing that he ever went to Germany, circa 1859, to attend the Heidelberg University School of Medicine, or had a brother who attended the United States Military Academy at West Point during the same period.

While it is possible that he fought in the Civil War, no Confederate or Union military records have been found for him. On two occasions he claimed to have served the Confederacy. During 1880 he would tell an Arizona reporter that he had been a "First Lieutenant in the 10th Texas Cavalry." By 1893, when talking to the San Francisco reporter, he more modestly claimed to have "entered the Confederate army as a bugler."

Leslie further complicated the claims of his Civil War service in 1900 when he wrote a newspaper tribute to Major General Henry Ware Lawton, in which he recalled that he "knew Lawton when he was a private, fighting his way through more than thirty battles of the Civil War." In order for this to be true, Leslie had to have served as a member of the Union forces.

Chapter 2

Buckskin Frank Enters Frontier History

Beyond his March 18, 1842, birthday in Texas nothing is really known of Nashville Franklyn Leslie's first twenty-seven years that can be supported with documentation. This all changed on July 11, 1869, when the *Daily Alta California*, a San Francisco newspaper, published the passenger list of the steamship *Portland*, owned by the Pacific Mail Steamship Company, which had docked in San Francisco. The list identified forty-four passengers by name and "26 others," who were not identified. Among the forty-four who were identified was a certain "N. F. Leslie."[1]

We know this person was a man, since all of the female passengers were listed with a "Miss" or "Mrs." preceding their names. While it can't be stated with certainty, it seems very probable that this "N. F. Leslie" was Nashville Franklyn Leslie. There is no record of Leslie remaining in San Francisco after the *Portland* docked in 1869. The sole mention of someone that *might* have been him, was when the May 31, 1871, issue of *San Francisco Chronicle* printed a lengthy list of unclaimed letters that included the name "Frank Leslie." The first known mention of Nashville

Franklyn "Frank" Leslie actually being a San Francisco resident doesn't appear until 1878.

It is possible that after the *Portland* docked, Leslie migrated to a mining camp in California or Nevada, but he could have gone anywhere. There is no record of him living in San Francisco prior to 1878. There are also no documents showing that Leslie was in Arizona earlier than 1880. Tom Horn would claim otherwise in his autobiography, in which he wrote that he, Leslie, and several others, were employed as scouts in Arizona during 1877, in the area that would later be the site of Tombstone. Horn claimed that he "had seven or eight good horses and a fine outfit, as did others of the scouts." He claimed Al Sieber was their leader, and named Archie McIntosh, Sam Bowman, Frank Monic, Charley Mitchell, Long Jim Cook—a man who was six-feet eight-inches tall—Frank Leslie, Frank Bennett, Sage, Merijilda Grijola, Jose Maria Yescus, and Big Ed Clark scouts or interpreters. Horn also noted "there were a good many packers. I think there were twenty-one of us in the bunch." Horn further recalled:

> We stayed around Tucson for a while that summer till Ed Schefflin [*sic*] came in from California and was getting an outfit at Tucson to go to where he had found some rich mineral a few years before that time. Schefflin and Sieber were well acquainted, and they had a talk. So we all concluded that we would go to this place as we had nothing else to do. Most all of the packers had gone to work "skinning" [driving] mules for some of the freighters, so that when we did finally pull out with Schefflin there were only about five or six of our original crowd.[2]

Tom Horn never said whether Leslie was among the "five or six of our original crowd." Lorenzo D. Walters in his 1928 book *Tombstone's Yesterday* had no problem including Leslie among the group of "five or six," when he decided to improve upon Horn's version. In this version, Walters came no closer to the correct spelling of Edward Schieffelin's name than Tom Horn had. Walters recorded that upon arrival at Tucson most of the gang obtained work with various freighting outfits until "only five or six of the original crowd" remained. On his return from California

Ed Schieffelin stopped in Tucson for the purpose of prospecting the country now known as the Tombstone Mining District. Buckskin Frank Leslie, Al Sieber, and Tom Horn joined him along with about sixty or more seasoned prospectors. They started for what they called "Cochise Country," as Cochise had been born in that country and had ruled it until the time of his death. After Cochise died, Geronimo became the leader of all the Apache, who quickly "engaged in keeping out the invaders." Six days after their start, they landed on the ground where now stands the town of Tombstone and where the Indians had killed Scheffelein's partner, one Lenox. Scheffelein, according to Tom Horn, stated that as the initial monument of his first claim was right at the grave of Lenox, he would call the camp Tombstone.[3]

The Horn/Walters accounts make for a great story, but historians now agree that there is absolutely no truth to it. Tom Horn's most recent biographer summed it up best when he wrote that "one of Horn's most ridiculous claims in his autobiography was that he, Sieber, ["Long Jim"] Cook, and other packers were with Edward Schieffelin when the latter made the silver discovery that led to the founding of the Tombstone Mining District."[4] Leslie's 1999 biographer also agreed that the Horn claim could be characterized as "ridiculous" when he observed "the discovery and early workings of Tombstone are among the best documented events in the history of the Territory. The two leading principals, Ed Schieffelin and Richard Gird, have left detailed, fascinating accounts; there is no room in the historical records for Tom Horn, Frank Leslie and others."[5]

If the story of Leslie and Tom Horn being in Arizona in 1877 has proven to be fiction, there is no question of Leslie's whereabouts the following year. He had returned to San Francisco by the time the 1878 *San Francisco City Directory* was published and listed him as a "barkeeper" employed at Thomas Boland's saloon at 311 Pine Street in San Francisco. Leslie's home address was given as 732 Howard Street.[6]

In the *San Francisco City Directory* for 1879 Leslie was listed as a "bookkeeper," which was almost certainly a typo for "barkeeper." He was employed by James P. Kerr and Thomas A. Jurado at an establishment called Kerr & Jurado's Saloon & Billiard Room on Hardie Place, near Kearny Street in San Francisco. In the 1879 directory Leslie's home address was given as 90 Third Street.[7]

In the 1878, 1879, and 1880 San Francisco city directories he was listed simply as "Frank Leslie," raising the question of whether the man in those directories and Nashville Franklyn Leslie were, in fact, the same individual. The definitive answer was provided by Leslie himself in 1893, when he was interviewed by W. H. Cameron of the *San Francisco Chronicle.* According to Cameron, "after the war Frank came West and at one time was a partner of the late James P. Kerr in a saloon on Hardie Place in this city."[8]

It is not known whether Leslie was inflating his own importance in the Hardie Place saloon when he told the reporter that he had been "a partner of the late James P. Kerr." By the time the 1880 *San Francisco City Directory* was published, Thomas A. Jurado was no longer connected with the business, which was now identified simply as "Kerr & Co." There was no mention of Leslie being a partner. Leslie was listed in the 1880 directory only as a "bartender," who was now living at 746 Folsom Street.[9]

It seems probable that Leslie had already left San Francisco by the time that the 1880 city directory was issued to the public. Leslie had decided to become just one of the many San Franciscans who left that city to try their luck in the boom town of Tombstone, Arizona. Accompanying Leslie to Tombstone was a fellow San Franciscan named William H. Knapp.[10] We know that Leslie and Knapp arrived in Tombstone very early in 1880, at the same time that some of the Wild West's most celebrated figures were also gathering there.

Leslie arrived in Tombstone looking like a sawed-off version of Buffalo Bill Cody, dressed in the buckskin attire of a scout. They called him "Buckskin Frank" from the moment he first set foot in the mining camp. Leslie stood only 5' 7" and weighed about 135 pounds but still managed to cut a dashing figure. When in town, he traded in the clothing of a frontiersman for the more fashionable attire of the San Franciscan that he had recently been. In order to live up to his sobriquet, Leslie allegedly accessorized his city attire with a fringed buckskin vest.

"Buckskin Frank" was known as "Frank Leslie" at least as far back as his listing as such in the 1878 *San Francisco City Directory.* This is at odds with the story told by a certain "Jim Brophy" to an Arizona newspaper reporter in 1934. According to that account, Brophy "knew Leslie in San Francisco but under the name of Korrigan. Entering a saloon in Tombstone where Leslie was tending bar, Brophy was surprised to see his acquaintance and yelled 'Hello, Korrigan, what are you doing here?' Korrigan turned his head quickly, then put his fingers to his lips . . . 'Jim, not so loud, I'm known here as Frank Leslie.' He was Leslie to Brophy from then on."[11]

Twenty years after this was written, after Jim Brophy had died, historian Philip J. Rasch tracked down Brophy's son and pointed out several things that were wrong with the "Korrigan" story. The best that Brophy's son could come up with was that perhaps the correct spelling should have been "Corrigan."[12]

On May 1, 1880, the *Tombstone Epitaph* began publishing daily and weekly editions. John Philip Clum, the founder of the *Epitaph*, was also appointed Tombstone's postmaster on June 4. Leslie's name would appear in the *Epitaph*, and other Tombstone papers, frequently that year, and in the years that followed. Around the time of the appointment of Clum as postmaster, Leslie was approached by a writer from a brand-new publication of a different type. It was called the *Arizona Quarterly Illustrated*, and they asked Leslie if he would be willing to grant them an interview. Leslie was glad to oblige, and provided the writer with this highly imaginative account of his life:

> N.F. Leslie is a character more frequently read about than met with in the ordinary walks of life. He is a native of Texas, and now about 37 years of age. He is a man who is thoroughly conversant with every phase of life, and familiar with all grades of society, having a

> natural taste for seeing for himself whatever is to be seen. He has since the age of twelve, been amid scenes of peril, and danger, and his life has been one of strange adventure. In 1861 he joined the Southern Army, and continued with it, till April 9th, 1865, at the time for the grand surrender, when he was attached to General Gordon's division, as First Lieutenant, in the 10th Texas Cavalry.
>
> At a later period, he attained great notoriety, as an Indian scout, and was known all over the plains, and on the frontiers, as "Buckskin Frank." From '70 to '73 he was Deputy Sheriff of Abalene [*sic*] and Elsworth [*sic*] counties, Kansas, under the notorious J.B. Hickock [*sic*] , or "Wild Bill." During this period, he took some of the longest and most daring rides of any man now living; oftimes his scalp was in dangerous proximity to the knife of a foe.
>
> At another time, he formed one of 50 prospectors, that left the southern portion of Colorado, of which four, besides himself, were all that returned, the balance being killed by Indians. Another time finds him a rough rider in Australia; next he became a [ship] pilot in the Fiji Islands. He has exhibited, as a fancy rifle shootist, in different parts of the world. At Tombstone, Dame Fortune has smiled upon him, and he is now on the right road to make a handsome provision for old age. He is, in manner, very pleasant, is an excellent conversationalist, and has the general bearing of a thorough gentleman.[13]

Leslie joined forces with his California friend William H. Knapp to open Knapp & Leslie's Cosmopolitan Saloon, located next to the Cosmopolitan Hotel at 409 Allen Street, which was owned and operated by forty-nine-year-old Carl Gustave Bilicke and his eighteen-year-old son Albert Clay Bilicke.[14] The 1880 United States Federal Census for Tombstone listed the saloon partners as being "Leslie, Frank, age 35 [*sic*], Saloon Keeper, born Texas" and "Knapp, William H., age 29, Saloon Keeper, born New York." Leslie was actually 38-years-old when the census was enumerated on June 3, 1880. It is significant that he told the enumerator that he was born in Texas.[15]

Twenty-three-year-old Mary Jane "May" Evans was employed at the Cosmopolitan Hotel as chambermaid when she married thirty-two-year-old Michael D. "Mike" Killeen on April 13, 1880. The ceremony was performed in the parlor of the Cosmopolitan by Rev. J.V. McIntyre. Chosen as witnesses were twelve-year-old Louisa Emma Bilicke and thirty-eight-year-old Nashville Franklyn Leslie. According to information on their wedding certificate, the bride and groom were both recent arrivals from Virginia City, Nevada.[16]

Something happened that caused the newlyweds to quickly separate. May's estranged husband remained very possessive about his wife, and when Leslie began paying too much attention to her, trouble was inevitable. It came on the evening of June 22, 1880.

Chapter 3

The Killing of Mike Killeen

On June 22, 1880, the Bilicke family had celebrated Albert Clay Bilicke's nineteenth birthday at their Cosmopolitan Hotel. The family had gone to bed by the time that Mrs. May Killeen and Buckskin Frank Leslie took their seats on the porch of the Bilickes' Cosmopolitan Hotel, following a night on the town. Suddenly a friend of Leslie's, George M. Perine, spotted Mike Killeen approaching and yelled a warning to Leslie.

Perine's warning came almost too late. Killeen fired two quick shots—both of which grazed Leslie's head. Killeen then sprang upon the dazed Leslie and proceeded to club him with a revolver. Leslie's ordeal came to an abrupt end when Mike Killeen was shot. The question was who fired the shot that mortally wounded Killeen? Leslie would testify that he killed Killeen. However, in his deathbed statement given to miner E.T. Packwood,[1] Mike Killeen asserted that it was actually George M. Perine who fired the fatal shot:

> At the ball I wanted to see my wife, I heard that she had gone home with Leslie, and when I was told she had gone home I went down to the hotel with the expectation of finding both of them in Leslie's room, but they were not there. Meanwhile I started towards the porch, having heard voices, and I thought it might be them. I got

> to the door of the porch and satisfied myself she and Leslie were sitting side by side, his arm around her waist. That settled it.
>
> I thought I would go off now. Started back again. Perine came along [with] pistol in hand and knowing him to be a particular friend of Leslie I looked for trouble as in the early part of the evening he went into Tasker & Hoke's and bought a box of cartridges and filled all chambers of his pistol and deposited the remainder of the box with me.
>
> I started away from the porch when Perine came along and yelled out, "Look out Frank, there is Mike," with that Leslie rose from his chair in a half standing position, pulling his pistol. He fired the pistol at me and I fired one shot at him. I saw I was in for it and I made a jump and caught the pistol and beat him over the head with mine, which I had in my hand at the time. I happened to look and saw Perine standing in the door with his pistol leveled at me. He pulled the trigger, which he repeated twice, firing in all three shots. By this time I had used up Leslie pretty well, then turned and jumped and caught Perine's pistol and did the same to him.
>
> By this time people commenced to congregate and I dropped this man, not thinking of my own wounds. All I knew was that I was shot in the nose somewhere. I fired two shots myself intentionally, and every time I would strike the pistol went off accidentally. Fired at Perine when he fired at me. One shot was at Perine and one at Leslie. Fired at Leslie when he pulled his revolver first and stood in a half stooping position.
>
> This was right after he first fired at me.[2]

Reports of the shooting involving Killeen, Leslie, and Perine were printed by papers from other states and territories, with often garbled results. The worst example was given by a Nevada newspaper called the *Reno Gazette-Journal*, which produced a record number of errors, within the space of four sentences, when it reported that "Mike Keller, barber of the Palace saloon, Tombstone, on the 23d inst. fired at Frank Leslie twice, making two scalp wounds. Leslie returned the fire and shot Keller in the breast and face, seriously wounding him. Keller says that a woman named Herin fired the shot that hit him in the breast, but Leslie denies that, and assumes all the responsibility. Jealousy was at the bottom of the trouble."[3]

After lingering for five days, Mike Killeen finally died on June 28, 1880. Following this, both Leslie and Perine were brought before the court on murder charges. Leslie claimed that he fired the fatal shot in self-defense and that Perine was not involved. The court accepted Leslie's version and both men were discharged.

As soon as he was free to go, Leslie went prospecting in the Dragoon Mountains with his friend Col. Roderick F. Hafford (1834-1900). Leslie and Hafford located what appeared to be a rich deposit of copper ore. They named their find "Copperopolis," and on July 1, 1880, filed their claim at the Pima County Recorder's Office. In the claim documents, Leslie was designated by Colonel Hafford as "my true and lawful attorney." The "Copperopolis" would be the first of several claims located by Leslie, along with various partners, in the section of Pima County that was soon to become Cochise County.[4]

After a respectful interval of eight days following her husband's death, the widow Killeen married Frank Leslie. Their marital status was made legal with a document that said "I certify that on the 6th day of July 1880 at Tombstone, the county of Pima, Territory of Arizona, N.F. Leslie and May Killeen both of Tombstone in said county were by me joined in marriage. [signed] James Reilly, J. P."[5]

Once again, for the second time within a ninety-day period, Mary Jane "May" Evans Killeen had been married in the parlor of the Cosmopolitan Hotel, just a few steps from the spot where her first husband had been killed in a shooting that involved her new husband. The witness standing up for Leslie was a certain "Colonel C. F. Hines." May once again chose Louisa Emma Bilicke as her witness. Louisa, now a teenager, had celebrated her thirteenth birthday during the three-month interval between the bride's two weddings.[6]

The *Epitaph* gave a glowing report concerning a new saloon that opened its doors in Tombstone on July 21, 1880. This establishment would play a prominent role in Leslie's career there. The article also provided an introduction to Milton Edward Joyce, who would be a key figure in Leslie's life and fortunes during most of Leslie's time in and around Tombstone during the 1880s. The *Epitaph* reported that for the past several weeks "the spacious corner building of the Vizinia & Cook Block" had been undergoing numerous finishing touches prior to when "Messrs. Joyce & Co.", described as "the genial proprietors" of the Oriental Saloon took over. The "portals" were thrown open and the public was permitted "to gaze upon the most elegantly furnished saloon this side of the Golden Gate. Twenty-eight burners suspended in neat chandeliers afforded an ample brilliancy, and the bright rays reflected from the many colored crystals on the bar sparkled like December iceling in the sunshine." Supposing this would impress the readers of the *Epitaph*, the editor took careful note of the saloon itself. He described it is as comprising two apartments, and to "the right of the main entrance is the bar beautifully carved, finished in white gilt and capped with a handsomely polished top. In the rear of this stand a brace of boards which are simply elegant and must be seen to be appreciated." This "brace of boards" were made for the Baldwin Hotel of San Francisco, but being too small, Mr. Joyce purchased them. The back apartment "was covered with a brilliant Brussels carpet, and suitably furnished after the style of a grand clubroom with conveniences for wily dealers in polished ivory." The editor could hardly contain himself in describing this marvelous business in Tombstone, writing that the "selection of furniture and fixtures displays an exquisite taste, and nothing seems to have been forgotten—even to a handsome stock of stationery." He was able to conclude his praise by stating that Tombstone "takes the lead" and offered "Messrs. Joyce & Co., our congratulations."[7]

The building that the Oriental Saloon was housed in was actually owned by James Vizina and Benjamin Cook. The Oriental's bar and restaurant were *leased* to Milton E. Joyce and a fellow San Franciscan named William C. Parker. When the 1880 United States Federal Census was taken in Tombstone the month prior to the opening of the Oriental, Milton Edward Joyce was described as being a thirty-three-year-old "miner," who was born in "Virginia."[8] This may have been a mistake on the enumerator's part, since numerous other records, including California census records, as well as voter registration lists for Arizona and California, are consistent in giving "New York" as Joyce's birthplace. While his birth date fluctuates on some of these records, 1847 would seem to be the correct year. Joyce came to California when he was fifteen, and briefly worked as a blacksmith in San Mateo County. By October 18, 1876, he was recorded on a California voter registration list as twenty-eight-year-old resident of San Francisco who was born in New York.[9] It is not known if Joyce and Leslie had known each other in San Francisco, before both of them turned up in Tombstone early in 1880. It wouldn't have mattered, since they were just two of the many San Franciscans who drifted into Tombstone that year.

The violence continued in Tombstone, but didn't involve Leslie. A man named T. J. Waters was shot and killed on Allen Street by E. L. Bradshaw on July 24, 1880. Three days later, Wyatt Earp was appointed deputy sheriff for the Tombstone district of Pima County under Sheriff Charles A. Shibell. On July 30, 1880, George W. Parsons wrote in his diary: "Still another man killed—Wilson—shot dead this a.m. by King, an anti-Chinese agitator who is at the head of a movement here to drive out the Chinese. Our town is getting a pretty hard reputation. Men killed every few days."[10] Thomas Wilson had been a recent arrival from San Francisco. Roger King was also a recent arrival, and known trouble-maker. Following the Wilson killing, a coroner's inquest was held and Leslie—identified in the record as "N.F. Leslie, scout" —gave this testimony:

> Was at my place of business at the Cosmopolitan Hotel; heard the shots fired went to the scene of the shooting about five minutes after; found a man dead; opened his shirt; saw a wound a few inches above the nipple of the left breast; returned to saloon; don't

> know the name of the man or who he was; did not see defendant present; saw none of the shooting.
>
> Saw the defendant about an hour prior to the shooting; time about 6 a.m. July 30th. Saw defendant in my saloon; he came in and asked me for cartridges; wanted them to fill the cylinder of a Colt's pistol. The defendant was much excited; was bleeding; said he had been beaten by someone; did not say by whom . . . do not know where defendant went upon leaving saloon; defendant said party beating him had also tried to rob him; and in endeavoring to prevent him his hand had been bruised; saw defendant's hand; it was skinned and bleeding.[11]

Five weeks later, on August 14, new developments caused the investigation of the Mike Killeen killing to be reopened. On that date W.T. Lowry swore out a warrant against George Perine charging him with murder. Morgan Earp tracked down Perine near the town of Richmond, and re-arrested him for the murder of Mike Killeen. A second examination, lasting nearly two weeks, was held before Justice James Reilly, who had recently wed Leslie and the widow Killeen. On August 24, Leslie provided this testimony, which was noteworthy for making no mention of Perine:

N. F. Leslie Sworn.

> On the night of 22d of June last I was sitting on the front porch of the Cosmopolitan Hotel, in company with Mrs. Killeen, who sat opposite me, and a few feet away. This was between 12 and 1 o'clock as near as I can recollect. I had just bid the lady good night, and was about to arise from the chair, when I heard a voice behind me say, "Take that, you s-- of a b----," and a shot was fired at the same time, the bullet from which struck me on the side of the head. I stood up immediately and found myself facing Mike Killeen. I was about to speak to him when the lady put her hand on some part of my coat behind me and spoke to me. What she said I could not understand at that moment. Killeen then fired the second shot, the ball striking me on the top of the head. When I saw him raise his hand to fire at me, as I imagined, I dropped to

my knees as quickly as I could, and catching him around the legs I threw him over my head, but one of the chairs on which Mrs. Killeen and I had been sitting kept him from falling. In getting up I put my hand on a big pistol which I had laid on the porch at my feet when first sitting down, but in trying to cock this pistol it slipped out of my hand.

I then stood up and grappled with Killeen. We struggled past the doorway, toward the west end of the porch, but did not quite reach the end. During this time Killeen was trying to get the point of his pistol toward me. I had a firm hold of his right hand with my left hand, and some part of his left side with my right hand. He forced the pistol from me at last, and stuck me on the top of the cheek with the muzzle of it. I let go of his side, and turned the pistol away from me as quickly as possible.

The pistol went off just then, and I saw Killeen's face distinctly by the flash. He swore and groaned directly when the pistol went off, saying "Oh, my God!" and snuffling as though struck in the face or nose. He staggered back, and I sank to the floor of the veranda. While in the act of rising to my feet, I drew a pistol from my right hip pocket with my right hand, and fired at the upper part of Killeen's body as he came toward me, I still being on my hands and knees, with my left hand being on the veranda floor.

I got to my feet and we clinched and struggled a little while. During the struggle I fired again, and we both fell. Killeen was the first on his feet, and made for the door, and went down the hallway. I then felt along the veranda for this big pistol, and found it at once. I then turned in the hallway after Killeen. He, Killeen, stopped some distance down the hallway and spoke. Upon seeing his hand raise as if to fire again, I fell on my knees and fired at him. He turned and ran out of the hallway. I struggled along after him, half blind with blood. On getting to the head of the stairs I heard officer [James W.] Bennett's voice asking me for the pistol. I sank down on the head of the stair way insensible—at least I don't recollect anything for a little while. I did not see the defendant

> Perine from the time I left him at the hall door until sometime after the shooting.[12]

The widow of Mike Killeen, now Mrs. Nashville Franklyn "Buckskin Frank" Leslie, also took the stand for the defense. Her testimony reveals no excitement or even a hint of the terror which she must have realized at the time. She related how on that night her then-husband was killed by her present husband, the twenty-second of June, sitting on the front porch of the Cosmopolitan Hotel, the time was after midnight, "[a]s best as she could remember." She was "in company" with Mr. Leslie when Mr. Killeen, her husband, stepped up "and called Mr. Leslie a bad name and fired." She continued, explaining how Leslie "rose to his feet facing Killeen." She then rose up and put her hand on Leslie, "begging him not to go further." The meaning of her "begging him not to go further" is not clear and apparently no one asked her to elaborate on that statement. When Killeen fired the second shot she recalled how she then ran to Albert Bilicke's room and told him "that Killeen had shot Leslie and he was now coming after me and for God's sake to save me." Young Bilicke went to the front porch and she went after him where they both saw Killeen and Leslie "scuffling." Albert Bilicke then went back to his room with Mrs. Leslie following him where he got his revolver and then went back to the porch a second time, again with Mrs. Killeen following. "When we reached the porch they were gone. . . . [if] Perine had been upon the porch while I was there I would have seen him. I am now the wife of Leslie."[13]

The examination of George M. Perine concluded on August 27, 1880. He was held until action could be taken by the grand jury at Tucson. Perine was then taken to Tucson by deputy sheriff Wyatt Earp, and spent the next two months in jail. When the grand jury met in October, it did not agree with the findings of the Tombstone judge. As far as the Tucson grand jury was concerned, Leslie had killed Mike Killeen in self-defense and there the matter ended.

During late September 1880, Leslie made his contribution to Arizona archaeology. A Tucson paper reported that "During a recent visit to Cachise [*sic*] Pass, Frank Leslie discovered five caves that had evidently at some time or other been the habitation of the Apaches. The inner walls were covered with paintings of scorpions, snakes, Indians, etc., in the manner similar to the painted rocks near Gila Bend."[14] Leslie returned to the Cosmopolitan Hotel, and his wife May, following his discovery of the five caves. The *Epitaph* of September 23, 1880, gave a list of "Hotel Arrivals at the Cosmopolitan," which included, "N.F. Leslie, Chiricahua Mountains."[15]

Late in September, Leslie filed a claim for a five-acre mill site where he and Col. Roderick F. Hafford had located the "Copperopolis" claim during late June. In the official record, this was described as the "Leslie Mill Site."[16] On September 29 a trip that Frank and May Leslie took to Tucson was covered by the *Arizona Daily Star*. It noted that "N.F. Leslie and wife are at the Palace."[17]

On October 11, 1880, John Henry "Doc" Holliday and Milton E. Joyce got into an argument at the Oriental Saloon. Doc, who was unarmed, left and returned with a pistol. Joyce spotted Doc first and quickly belted Doc in the head with a pistol. Doc somehow managed to get off a couple of shots. Joyce was shot through his left hand, while the other bullet from Doc's gun struck Joyce's partner, William C. Parker, in the big toe of his left foot. City Marshal Fred White and officer James Bennett separated Joyce and Holliday and took them into custody. The following day Doc plead guilty to assault and battery. He was fined $20 plus $11.25 in court costs.

The fight between Holliday and Joyce may not seem to have been an even match, since it is well known that Doc Holliday suffered from tuberculosis, while Joyce had once worked as a blacksmith. The fact was, however, that at this point in his life Milton E. Joyce was tubercular as well. Both Joyce and Holiday would die from the disease, just two years and three weeks apart. For a time it was thought that Joyce might have to have the hand that had been shot by Holliday amputated. It turned out that he didn't and on October 27, 1880, the *Epitaph* reported that "M.E. Joyce is now considered out of danger, and will not lose the use [of] his hand, which was at one time feared."[18]

"Curly Bill" Brocius on October 28, 1880, shot City Marshal Fred White in the groin during a scuffle. Deputy Sheriff Wyatt Earp, who was standing nearby, took Curly Bill into custody. City Marshal White died from his wounds but before he died, White said the shooting was accidental and Curly Bill was exonerated.

A Tucson newspaper published a list of twenty "Mining Locations" that were filed at the Recorder's Office in Tombstone on October 29, 1880. Among the twenty were three named claims, registered by "N.F. Leslie," along with fellow "locators" that included his friend and business partner William H. Knapp. N.F. Leslie and James A. Burrows registered the first claim, "Village," on September 1, 1880. N.F. Leslie, William H. Knapp, C.M. Gratton and James Burrows registered the second claim as "Abliane" on September 3. The final claim, registered on October 2, was called "Big Buck," and listed as locators N.F. Leslie and "James A. Burruss," who was probably Burrows.[19]

Wyatt Earp resigned as deputy sheriff of Pima County on November 9, 1880. Earp resigned in order to support the candidacy of Robert H. "Bob" Paul, who was running for sheriff against Earp's boss, the incumbent Sheriff Charles A. Shibell. On the day after Earp's resignation, Frank Leslie rode into Tombstone following a trip to New Mexico. The *Tombstone Nugget* reported that "Frank Leslie returned Wednesday [November 10] evening from a scouting trip into southeastern New Mexico, visiting all the mining camps of that section. He reported everything there as looking prosperous but to use his own words, 'There's no Tombstone there.'"[20]

At the end of November 1880, Leslie was appointed as a special deputy sheriff, with a very limited area to patrol. The minutes of Tombstone's "Common Council" gave these details of his appointment: "Monday, November 29, 1880: On motion of Comstock, seconded by Jones, Frank

Leslie was granted power of arrest on the premises of the Oriental Saloon."[21]

As the year drew to a close, a two year-old child was run over by a buggy on Fremont Street, but somehow survived with few injuries. On December 14, 1880, John P. Clum, editor of the *Epitaph*, made the acerbic observation that "Fremont street seems to have been selected as a speeding ground for our fast trotters. Children should be kept out of the street, as it often happens that a valuable buggy is ruined from running over a child—and buggies cost money."[22]

Chapter 4

1881—Tombstone's Crowded Year

On January 4, 1881, John P. Clum was elected mayor of Tombstone. Ten days later, Michael O'Rourke—known as "Johnny-Behind-the-Deuce" — shot and killed Henry Schneider in nearby Charleston. On the same day that Schneider was killed, Frank Leslie took the precaution of adding to his personal arsenal—as this letter illustrates:

Tombstone, A.T.

Jan 14th 1881

> Colts Patent F.A. Com
>
> Gentlemen
>
> I want a pistol made as follows,
>
> Colts Frontier Model to take Winchester Cartridges 44 cal., the revolver to have a twelve inch barrel, browned, superior finished throughout with carved Ivory handle. Also send scabberd [*sic*] and belt with everything complete for carrying & cleaning the

Pistol answer soon as convenient, stating price and when I can have Pistol by Wells Fargo & oblige

Yours Respt

CAPT N.F. LESLIE

Box 28

Tombstone

Arizona Territory

P.S. I want this pistol to be first class in every respect.[1]

One of the most oft-told (but unproven) tales concerning Leslie and his weaponry relates how Leslie employed a Tombstone silversmith to weld a large screw head that protruded ¾-inch from the frame on the side of his Colt .45 so that it fit into a slot on a metal clip attached to his gunbelt. This allowed Leslie to make a pivot-shot from the hip, which he allegedly did with deadly accuracy. In order for this story to be true, Leslie would have had to have been unusually prescient. Louis S. Flatau patented an identical device, known as the "Bridgeport Rig," in 1882. It was manufactured by the Bridgeport Gun Implement Company of Bridgeport, Connecticut, and is sometimes called the "Gillett Rig," since Texas Ranger James B. Gillett used the device. Gillett would note that a Colt Peacemaker could be drawn quickly by sliding it in a straight line from its clip, and be fired even faster by leaving it attached and just swiveling the pistol.

John Harris Behan became the first sheriff of Cochise County, Arizona, on February 10, 1881. There is no known record of Frank Leslie's whereabouts when Luke Short killed Charlie Storms, outside the Oriental Saloon on February 25, 1881. The gunfight happened within inches of the spot where Leslie would kill Billy Claiborne the following year. Today, in Tombstone, a plaque marks the site of those two celebrated gunfights.

On March 15, 1881, an attempt was made to rob the Kinnear & Co. stage on a lonely stretch of road between Contention City and Drew's Station. Eli "Bud" Philpot, the driver, and Peter Roerig, a passenger, were killed during the attempted holdup. That night an all-star posse formed and rode off in pursuit of the robbers. Its members included Sheriff John Behan, "Buckskin Frank" Leslie, Bat Masterson, and Virgil, Wyatt, and Morgan Earp. The stage robbers were believed to have been Bill Leonard, Jim Crane, Harry Head and Luther King The posse caught up with Luther King on March 19.

The day before the posse caught up with King—Friday, March 18, 1881—had been Leslie's thirty-ninth birthday. That milestone was noted by the *Arizona Weekly Citizen*, with a report that said "Frank Leslie, the well known scout *who was with General Custer* [authors' italics], celebrated his thirty-ninth birthday last Friday."[2] The claim that Leslie had served with Custer would be made on other occasions—but no record of that service has been found.

Tombstone's celebrated diarist, George W. Parsons, noted in an entry for March 22, 1881, that "another party started out today for [the stage] robbers—just three or four men but amongst them two of the best trailers and plainsmen in the U.S., so said – F. Leslie and Breakenridge."[3] The posse that Parsons referred to was led by Sheriff John H. Behan and its members were Marshall Williams, William M. Breakenridge, Ed Gorman and Buckskin Frank Leslie.

In his 1928 memoir, William M. Breakenridge recalled that "this was my first trip with Frank Leslie. He was the life of the party, he had a good voice and sang well, told good stories, never complained of being tired, was always ready to go. He was a much better companion in the country than he was in town."[4] The *Tombstone Epitaph* later reported that Breakenridge and Leslie were paid $83 by the County Supervisor's Board for their services as scouts for the posse.[5]

On April 13, 1881, Doc Holliday walked into the Oriental and threatened the life of Milton E. Joyce. Before any trouble could happen, Sheriff Behan arrested both men. Joyce quickly swore out a warrant for "threats against life." Holliday was then hauled off to Justice Albert O. Wallace's court.[6]

A raging inferno destroyed sixty-six stores, saloons and assorted other businesses, within a four-block area, before the fire was contained on June 22, 1881. Chief of Police Ben Sippy had left Tombstone, prior to the fire, and had never returned. On June 28 the city council appointed Virgil Earp as the new chief of police. Soon afterward, Leslie also tried his hand at law enforcement when he filed a bond and took an oath as a deputy sheriff of Cochise County on July 1, 1881, reporting to Sheriff John H. Behan.[52] Two days after his appointment the *Tombstone Nugget* reported that Leslie was departing "for a trip of several weeks duration to the country eastward of us." Leslie was headed to the New Mexico ranch of John Plesent Gray, where he expected to find Jim Crane, one of the suspects in the March 15 stage holdup in which Eli "Bud" Philpot was killed. Years later, in his memoirs, John Plesent Gray recalled of Leslie's visit that it turned out to be peaceful, but could have turned ugly. The incident occurred in Gray's Animas Valley Ranch where Jim Crane was an occasional visitor. Leslie must have known this and went to the Gray Ranch to arrest Crane. It was no secret and Leslie informed Gray what his mission was: arrest Crane and deliver him to jail in Tombstone on the charge of stage robbing. Typically Crane would arrive at the ranch around noon to have lunch. It was part of the unwritten code of western hospitality to provide minimum food and water for man and beast. Neither discussed the possibility of what would happen if Crane resisted arrest. Gray recalled telling Leslie: "I did not think he would be able to arrest Jim without killing him and that I objected to any such method being sprung at our house. Both men would be our dinner guests and I expected that hospitality to be undisturbed by either party." Gray was grateful that his "warning was not necessary." Leslie was not afraid of Crane, but he respected ranchman Gray. The next portion of Gray's memoir is revealing:

> Jim Crane rode up at his usual time on a fine saddle mule, unmistakably a refugee from some army post. And as dinner was ready, I asked both in to the meal. It happened we three were alone, except for our old cook, Moody. Jim packed his carbine—a short Sharps rifle—into the cook tent and sat down on Leslie's right, with the gun across his lap and the muzzle in Frank's direction. I don't think any of us relished that meal much, and I know I should have preferred to be elsewhere. As might have been expected, all of us were on edge, but no sign of conflict appeared.
>
> Leslie did not even mention the purpose of his mission, but simply said that he must start for Tombstone at once. Immediately after lunch he mounted his horse, held out his hand to me to bid me good-bye, and said in a low voice so Jim wouldn't hear, "Tell Jim if they want him someone else will have to serve the warrant." When I repeated this to Jim he simply smiled and said, "I guess so." I heard later that Leslie had reported back to his [Sheriff Behan's] office that he could not find his man.[8]

Jim Crane was one of five Americans who were ambushed and killed, by Mexicans, in Guadalupe Canyon on August 13, 1881. The others were Newman Haynes "Old Man" Clanton, Bill Lang, Charles "Bud" Snow, and nineteen-year-old Dixie Lee "Dick" Gray.

On August 20 the *Tombstone Daily Nugget* reported that "Frank Leslie has returned to Tombstone from a two months' sojourn in southwestern New Mexico."[9] On his return to Tombstone from New Mexico, Leslie passed through Guadalupe Canyon and was one of the first to happen upon the scene of the August 13 massacre. Later, at a place called "Blackwater," Leslie "found the bodies of three dead Mexicans, but recently killed, which could indicate that retribution had commenced."[10]

On October 1, 1881, Geronimo and Naiche (son of the late Cochise) escaped from the San Carlos reservation with an estimated 400 other Apaches. On October 5 Mayor John P. Clum gathered a posse to go after Geronimo and the others who had fled the reservation. Clum's posse included Virgil, Wyatt, and Morgan Earp as well as Sheriff John Harris Behan, Deputy Sheriff William M. Breakenridge, and George W. Parsons among others. The posse failed to track the Apaches down.

On October 26, 1881, the celebrated shootout near the O.K. Corral took place, which resulted in the two McLaury brothers and Billy Clanton being killed and Virgil and Morgan Earp being seriously wounded. Three days later Chief of Police Virgil Earp was suspended from his position, while an investigation was conducted. On October 31, Justice Wells Spicer began a hearing to see if the Earp brothers and Doc Holliday should be charged with murder and brought to trial.

Two weeks later it was announced that Leslie, who was doing very well financially, had opened a second saloon, located directly across Allen Street from Knapp & Leslie's Saloon. The *Epitaph* of November 13 reported that "Mr. N.F. Leslie has just re-opened Jack Doling's old stand as a first class saloon. He will keep nothing but the choicest brands of wines, liquors and cigars, and considering his popularity and the prestige of the place, he will undoubtedly secure a large share of public patronage."[11]

It was during November 1881 that a baby was suddenly, and unexpectedly, added to the Leslie household. The eight-month-old baby, born in Tombstone on March 19, 1881, was named Carlotta Crabtree. Her parents were a single woman named Annie Leopold and John Ashcroft "Jack" Crabtree, the ne'er-do-well brother of the celebrated actress and comedienne Lotta Crabtree. At the time of the baby's birth, Jack Crabtree was running a livery stable in partnership with a man named Ed Bullock. In November, Jack Crabtree suddenly deserted Annie and the baby. Annie Leopold begged May Leslie to look after the infant, while she tried to track down Jack Crabtree. When it became clear that neither parent would be returning to Tombstone, May somehow convinced Ed Bullock, Jack Crabtree's recent business partner, to adopt the baby, which he did. Forty-five years later May Leslie would be a witness in a celebrated trial involving the grown-up Carlotta Crabtree.[12]

Nashville Franklyn Leslie was very much a member of the Tombstone community in ways not usually associated with a gunfighter. When the need arose, he served as a volunteer for the local "Hook and Ladder Company," and even served on a committee for a dance that the fire department was planning. The *Epitaph* reported that "at a meeting of the Hook and Ladder Company, held last evening [December 7, 1881], the following committee were appointed on the ball to be given January 2, 1882: R.S. Hatch, Howard Lee, G. Spangenburg, Dan Lynch, M.E. Joyce, P. Holland, N.F. Leslie, W.A. Freese, W.M. Breakenridge, W.E. Ludlow, A.C. Bilicke, Frank Hereford, W.W. Hubbard, W. Baron and W.A. Cuddy, who are requested to meet this afternoon in Judge Wallace's court room."[13]

The Benson night stage was attacked on December 14, 1881. It was alleged that the attack was an attempt on the life of Mayor John P. Clum who was one of the passengers. Clum was not harmed in the incident. Frank Leslie experienced a threat of a different kind as 1881 drew to a close. The *Tombstone Tribune* reported that Leslie was one of "our several prominent citizens [who] had received letters from some mysterious person, or persons, ordering them to leave town within a stated period." The *Tombstone Tribune* went on to say that, in Leslie's case, the warning advised "Frank Leslie—You will settle your business and leave town as soon as you can, or take the consequence." The *Tribune* concluded its report by stating that "Mr. Leslie desires to ask the authors reasons for his leaving town, and he will listen, but states he will not leave town. We hope for the good of the fair name of Tombstone, that these are merely jokes, perpetrated by Tombstone's many practical jokers."[14] Apparently is was some sort of practical joke, since there were no further reports of threatening letters.

As the year 1881 drew to a close, the *Weekly Epitaph* reported that "M. E. Joyce was arrested for disturbing the peace, by Sheriff Behan and fined $15 and costs."[15] Nine days after this report, on December 28, 1881, Virgil Earp was ambushed on Fifth Street, between the Oriental Saloon and the Golden Eagle Brewery. Virgil survived, but lost the use of his left arm after several inches of shattered bone had to be removed. He had brothers to avenge his loss.

Chapter 5

Leslie the "Masher"

Leslie rang in the new year by locating three mining claims on January 1, 1882. The trio of claims were located close to each other near the Dragoon Mountains. The claims were called "Kansas King," "Copper King," and "Moira." His partner in these claims was Col. Roderick F. Hafford. The three claims were all registered in Tombstone three days after they were located. Leslie signed himself as "Capt. N.F. Leslie" on each of the documents, while Colonel Hafford didn't bother using his military title.[1] Leslie was also the one-third owner of the "Leslie Mine," which was located very close to Tombstone. That venture didn't work out and on January 13, Leslie, along with his two partners, quit-claimed the property to H. Solomon for the sum of one dollar. [2]

January 1882 would prove to be a busy month for other notable Tombstone residents. John P. Clum lost his re-election bid for mayor of Tombstone on January 3. On January 17, John Ringo confronted Doc Holliday, who was standing with Wyatt Earp on a Tombstone street, and challenged him to a duel. Before any blood could be shed, Police Chief David Butler Neagle arrested Holliday and Earp while officer James Flynn arrested John Ringo. Holliday and Ringo were each fined $30. Earp was not charged and was released.

On January 10, 1882, the *Epitaph* reported that Lou Rickabaugh and Richard Clark had sold out their interests in the Oriental Saloon to Milton E. Joyce.[3] At this time Leslie seemed content to participate in civic-oriented pursuits. He continued to serve as an active member of the volunteer "Hook and Ladder Company" in Tombstone. He even agreed to be one of the acts doing a vaudeville-style turn in a fundraiser for the fire department, as described in this not-so-subtle announcement:

> ALL CITIZENS TAKE NOTICE
>
> That the delegates of the fire department of the city of Tombstone will immediately proceed to levy an assessment on each property owner of our city, to compel each of them to put up for at least one ticket for the benefit of the fire department, and will insist upon their attending the grand benefit at Schieffelin Hall, on Monday [February 6, 1882] evening next. No percentage for collection; one dollar pays the bill; reserved seats, one half more. Get your reserved seat early and come early; don't neglect the families.
>
> This is the grandest entertainment ever given in Tombstone. The following parties, in addition to the Wallace sisters, have volunteered for the occasion: Mrs. Lottie Hutchison, Messrs. Burns and Trayers, Messrs. Mulligan and Sheehan, Mr. F.E. Brooks and Mr. N.F. Leslie.[4]

During the early morning hours of March 16, 1882, Leslie got into an argument with a man named James Floyd in the Oriental Saloon. Later that day the *Tombstone Epitaph* reported that "Leslie had some words with Floyd in the saloon and a tussle ensued when Mr. [E.H.] Dean, who was [tending bar] on the night watch, pitched them into the street, where the row continued until Leslie drew his revolver and struck Floyd on the head, the revolver going off from the concussion."[5]

The *Tombstone Nugget* provided additional details of the Leslie-Floyd encounter reporting that "about 3 o'clock this morning an altercation occurred in the Oriental Saloon between 'Buckskin' Frank Leslie and a man named Floyd, which resulted in a slight amount of pistol practice on the part of the former. Neither party was seriously hurt and both were 'run in' by officer [James] Kenny."[6]

Nashville Franklyn "Buckskin Frank" Leslie celebrated his fortieth birthday on March 18, 1882. That evening Morgan Earp was assassinated while he was playing a game of billiards with Bob Hatch in Tombstone. Frank Stilwell, Pete Spence, and Florentino Cruz were considered the likely suspects in Morgan Earp's murder.

The Leslie-Floyd difficulty had a peaceful resolution on March 20, 1882, when "the case of the Territory against F. Leslie, charged with assault and battery, was called before Judge Wallace this morning. James Floyd, the prosecuting witness, withdrew the complaint, whereupon the case was dismissed." [7] On the same day that James Floyd withdrew his complaint against Leslie, the body of Frank Stilwell was found riddled with bullets in a Tucson railroad yard. This was the first killing in the so-called Earp "Vendetta Ride." Florentino Cruz would be next on March 22, followed by "Curly Bill" Brocius on March 24, 1882.

General William Tecumseh Sherman made a visit to Tombstone during early April of 1882. We can only wonder how Leslie, who claimed to have served as a Confederate soldier, felt about this visit. Certainly Leslie's friend Milton E. Joyce had no issues concerning Sherman's visit, and was, according to the *Epitaph*, designated the Grand Marshal of the parade that was to be held in Sherman's honor. The *Epitaph* advised that "those societies that intend taking part in the procession at the reception of Gen. Sherman are requested to leave word with the marshal of the day, Mr. M.E. Joyce, at the Oriental, at once, so that he may assign them a place in the procession. Mr. Joyce will name his aids tomorrow. Let the affair be the grandest in the history of Tombstone." [8]

A crowd gathered in Tombstone on April 30, 1882, and Leslie would be "loudly called for" by the crowd. The following day, the *Epitaph* ran an article headlined "The Indians Must Go," which described why Leslie was in demand by the crowd. According to this report there was "a rather extensive crowd collected on the corner of Allen and Fifth streets" answering to the call for a meeting. Judge Peel was called to make some remarks and "delivered an impassioned speech, stating that the only way to advance the interests of Arizona was to clean all the Indians out bag and baggage." He stated that Frank Leslie, whom he described as "an old time scout and plainsman, would lead a party of volunteers." Leslie did not disappoint the "extensive crowd" and stated "that he would go with one man or a hundred, on horseback or on foot." On motion of Judge Peel, a resolution appointing J.D. Kinnear and Frank Leslie canvassers for volunteers was passed. Both "entered on their duties immediately, Mr. Kinnear receiving subscriptions and Leslie the names of volunteers. Leslie headed the subscription with $100, and Kinnear followed suit. Several handsome subscriptions were handed in and thirty men subscribed themselves willingly to accompany Leslie on a scouting expedition."[9]

The *Tombstone Nugget*, in their report of the gathering, boosted the amount of Leslie's cash contribution and offered some interesting ideas concerning his résumé as a scout. Judge Peel's remarks included the statement to "the assemblage" that "the only thing that remained to be done was to hunt the Indians down to the last one." It would be a war of extermination, according to the reports of both Tombstone newspaper editors. Frank Leslie, "a scout of twenty-one years experience, and who well knew the mountain retreats of the Indians, was ready to lead a company of men to the lurking places of the wily foe." Frank Leslie and J.D. Kinnear were appointed a committee to solicit volunteers and supplies. Leslie headed the list with $150 and succeeded in raising about $700 in money.[10]

The amount of Leslie's contribution of $150 may not seem particularly impressive to twenty-first-century readers—until, using an inflation calculator, one discovers that $150 in 1882 dollars is the equivalent of $3,301.90 in 2017 dollars. The claim of Leslie being "a scout of twenty-one years experience" is also interesting. This would date Leslie's scouting activities back to 1861: the first year of the Civil War. The *Epitaph* also ran a related article, headlined "War Rumors" on May 1, which provided further information and warned about possible threats from the Indians:

> The town has been full of rumors of Indian massacres on the right hand and the left all day, but none of them could be traced to any authentic or reliable source, with the exception of the killing of James near Antelope Springs. Early in the day it was reported that three men had been killed on the Bisbee trail, but that was soon exploded, for at three o'clock in the morning a party of six or eight men, among whom were W.H. Savage, Gus Williams, Frank Leslie and Sam Hardie, arrived direct over the trail. . . . The rangers, who came in from a week's scout, will leave for the scene of the hostilities in the Sulphur Spring valley and Chiricahuas in the morning. It is neither safe nor wise for small parties to go out into the mountains at this time. An ounce of prevention is worth any amount of cure in a case of this kind. [11]

Tombstone's second great fire swept through the town on May 26, 1882. It was believed to have started at the Tivoli Saloon on Allen Street and spread quickly to other buildings. The total losses from the disaster were estimated at $500,000: nearly three times the amount lost in the first fire of June 22, 1881. Among the many buildings totally destroyed in this second fire were the Cosmopolitan Hotel and Knapp & Leslie's Cosmopolitan Saloon. The partners decided against rebuilding, and William H. Knapp decided to try his luck elsewhere in Arizona.[12] Leslie took a job tending bar at the Oriental Saloon, one of the few buildings not completely gutted by the conflagration.

The dictionary describes the slang term of "masher" as being "a man who makes unwanted sexual advances, often in public places and typically to women he does not know." During early June 1882 Leslie had signed on as an enumerator for a local census with the express purpose of going door-to-door and meeting numerous women that he did not know. According to the *Epitaph* "some time ago a Tombstone newspaper referred to Mr. Leslie, one of the census enumerators as a 'masher' and intimated that he took the appointment for the purpose of practicing at that peculiar business. Some days ago he rapped at the door of a Fourth Street residence. A lady with rotund features peeped through the window to see who was the caller, and recognizing the official, was heard to say, 'Patrick, get the club, the masher is comin.' "[13]

Chapter 6

The Death of John Ringo

John Yoast, an old Texas friend, found the corpse of John Ringo in a clump of black oaks across Turkey Creek near Arizona's Morse Canyon. It was the fourteenth of July 1882. A group of men promptly gathered and wrote and signed a "statement for the information of the Coroner and Sheriff of Cochise Ct. A.T." After writing their statement, a grave was dug, and Ringo was buried close to the spot where his body was found. In reporting the event, the *Tombstone Weekly Epitaph* headlined Ringo's death a "probable suicide."[1]

There have been many, then and now, who have refused to accept the suicide verdict, insisting that Ringo was killed by someone else. Several alleged Ringo killers have been offered over the years—including Buckskin Frank Leslie. Walter Noble Burns was one of the earliest writers to mention a possible Leslie connection in his 1927 book *Tombstone: An Iliad of the Southwest.* Burns wrote that it was "Soon after Ringo's death" that "a rumor became rife in Tombstone" that Frank Leslie had murdered him. Burns suggested that the story may have originated "merely in Leslie's reputation as a heartless killer." Apparently it was known (or believed) that Leslie had followed Ringo "out of town." Some claimed that William Floyd "Billy" Claiborne had identified Leslie as the man who murdered him, and further that "it was believed that Leslie had boasted of the deed." Burns of course did not identify those who shared with him the rumors; he points out that "[s]uch braggadocio would have been very dangerous; confessed murderers were going over the road to Yuma even in those lawless times. Old timers can remember no such boasts. If Leslie ever said he killed Ringo, he must have made the statement in whispered confidence only to his closest friends. Leslie had no cause to kill Ringo, as far as anyone knew. No one had ever heard of any quarrel between them. To all appearances, the two men were friends. The manner of Ringo's death seemed to preclude the possibility of Leslie's having killed him. It is certain Ringo met death while sitting in the forks of the tree. The spattered brains proved that beyond question. And the single empty chamber in Ringo's six-shooter seemed to prove that he had killed himself. But the story that Leslie murdered him remained definite and insistent. It passed into tradition, and most people in that country believe it implicitly today."[2] It is clear that Walter Noble Burns wanted the death of Ringo "both ways" —there was enough evidence to "prove" that he committed suicide, yet the story of his being murdered was believed "implicitly" then.

One of those who would "believe it implicitly" at that time was Lorenzo D. Walters who authored a book called *Tombstone's Yesterday* that was released in 1928. In his book, Walters wrote: "The next that was heard of John Ringo was when Buckskin Frank Leslie rode into town and informed the authorities that he had met John Ringo and they had fought it out and he had killed Ringo. . . . A coroner's jury verdict rendered on the ground, stated that he [Ringo] had come to his death as the result of a self-inflicted wound. This reason was generally accepted as the cause of his demise, in spite of the very vehement declaration of Buckskin Frank Leslie that he was responsible for his death; that he met Ringo and Ringo had shot at him and missed and that he had shot and killed him."[3]

William Milton Breakenridge, who knew both Leslie and Ringo in Tombstone, took a differing view in his own 1928 book, writing that

"Frank Leslie tried to curry favor with the Earp sympathizers by claiming that he met Ringo and had to kill him in self-defense, but the evidence proved this to be a lie. We all knew that Leslie would not care to tackle him even when he was drunk."[4] Wyatt Earp and his companions had left Arizona nearly three months before Ringo died. Given that fact, Breakenridge's assertion that "Leslie tried to curry favor with the Earp sympathizers" by claiming to have killed Ringo is nonsense. Those "sympathizers," and Earp himself, were long gone when Ringo died.

Fred Dodge was another contemporary of Ringo and Leslie who knew both men well. In a September 30, 1929, letter to Stuart N. Lake, Dodge wrote: "Frank Leslie did not kill John Ringo. Those two and myself were together a couple of days before Ringo was found dead. Ringo was found by Pony Deal and someone else that I do not, at this time, remember. They were coming in from the opposite side to where we were. In the intervening time I saw Frank Leslie several times—one night we stayed over on the White River together—and he had no possible chance to get to where Ringo was found and back before the news of the killing came in."[5]

Despite the total lack of evidence that would show that Leslie killed Ringo, there would be those who still insisted that he did. Arguably the most notorious individual making that claim was a one-time Tombstone resident named William Aurelius "Billy" King (1856–1945) whose memoirs, dictated to Charles Leland Sonnichsen, were published in 1942 under the title *Billy King's Tombstone.* According to King it was not long after Billy Claiborne was dead and buried when Ringo rode into town "and put on the usual show. When he was feeling his liquor enough, he stood up to Frank Leslie and demanded to know if he had ever shot anybody in front."

These were fighting words, and anyone witnessing the exchange might expect Leslie to answer the question with a challenge to fight. But then there were only words instead of gunfire. "I take them as they come," replied Frank. "Would you like to do anything about it?" They bickered around for a while, but at last Johnny rode off without burning any powder. Later that day some cowboys at the Stockton Ranch out in the Dragoon Mountains noticed a riderless horse "drifting" up to the house with the bridle down and a Winchester on the saddle. They ran him into the corral and started to backtrack him. About sundown they found his owner dead in a little canyon in the foothills. It proved to be John Ringo. He was sitting in the crotch of a scrub-oak tree with one boot off as if he had been getting ready to take a nap. There was a bullet hole between his eyes. About the time they found the body, Frank Leslie rode into the back gate of the O.K. Corral at Tombstone, his horse white with lather. He said he had been giving the "critter a hard run to take some of the ginger out of him." King, who clearly kept his ears and eyes to the ground to be knowledgeable of all things, claimed that the Stockton Ranch hands testified there were no tracks except those of Ringo between the scrub oak in which Ringo was sitting and the road. The result of this testimony was that Ringo had committed suicide. But then King's version seemingly contradicted this with this statement: "these same Stockton cowboys said they had seen hoof prints of a shod horse on the road not more than twenty feet from the body. Adding everything up, including the fact that Frank's horse was shod, everybody had a suspicion which he kept to himself. But it blew up Frank's reputation still more and brought him to the peak of his career."[6]

Despite all of the latter-day claims that Ringo was killed by Leslie, the findings of the coroner's jury were not challenged in 1882. No one, including Buckskin Frank Leslie, would ever officially be charged with killing him.

Early in September 1882, Leslie and Col. Roderick F. Hafford sold their interest in the Copperopolis claim, on the east side of the Dragoon Mountains, to Bartholomew McGlynn for one hundred dollars.7

On September 23, 1882, the *Tombstone Weekly Epitaph* reported that "at the Democratic Convention at Schieffelin Hall the committee on Organization and Order of Business appointed H.F. Price and Leslie as Sergeants at Arms." [8] The following month was also quiet for Leslie, and one of his rare press notices for that period described his coming to Tombstone on October 6, 1882. According to the *Epitaph*, "Frank Leslie came in from Sulphur Spring valley last evening. He has been as far as the Swisshelms, where he reports an abundance of game of the larger variety, deer, antelope, bear and a few Indian signs."[9]

The routine, almost mundane, press notices that Leslie was then receiving ended the following month when Leslie became front page news—in Tombstone, and elsewhere—because of his involvement in what was arguably one of the most famous gunfights in Wild West history. Unlike the group affair that happened the previous year, near the O.K. Corral, Leslie's showdown would be strictly mano a mano.

Chapter 7

The Killing of Billy Claiborne

Leslie was still employed at the Oriental when he became the last man standing in one of Tombstone's celebrated gunfights. For some time, twenty-two-year-old William Floyd "Billy" Claiborne had been one of Leslie's numerous friends. That friendship came to a sudden and violent end when Leslie shot and killed Claiborne on November 14, 1882. A lot of nonsense has been published concerning the cause of this gunfight. It had absolutely nothing to do with Claiborne's attempting to avenge Leslie's supposed killing of John Ringo four months earlier. That story is pure fiction. Leslie did not kill Ringo, and Claiborne probably couldn't have cared less that Ringo died—or how he died.

Billy Claiborne's death at Frank Leslie's hands can be traced to the results of a bitter election that happened exactly one week earlier. At the center of the electoral bitterness that pervaded Tombstone was Police Chief David Butler Neagle, one of three candidates for sheriff of Cochise County. The *Epitaph* was clearly not supporting Neagle in the election and opined that "it required a little over $2,000 to elect Neagle marshal [police chief] last January, and at that time, as now, he claimed that he controlled the miners. In that election he received a few over 500, in a vote of less than 1,300. He is not as strong today as he was then, and many who worked for him and spent their money to secure his election will do all in their power to defeat him for sheriff. Now there are nearly 2,000 voters registered in Tombstone, and at the same ratio as last spring he will not receive more than a third of them, which will defeat him in spite of every effort he or his friends may make."[1]

The *Epitaph* wasn't far off the mark in their vote tally prediction for the November 7, 1882, election for sheriff. When the votes were counted, Jerome L. Ward was declared the winner with 1,096 votes. David Butler Neagle came in second with 835, and was closely followed by Larkin W. Carr with 802. Neagle went beyond just being a sore loser, and physically attacked Milton E. Joyce, holding him responsible for his loss. Neagle and several of his "strikers" attacked M. E. Joyce just before the polls closed. Joyce was challenging a "repeater" (someone voting more than once) which he had a perfect right to do when he was kicked to the ground. His friends attempted to rescue him but not before he was kicked several more times. Joyce was able to hold onto Neagle and dragged him out into the street. Finally citizens managed to separate Joyce and Neagle before serious trouble developed. Even Neagle's "best friends" commented that his action was totally out of place.2

The political arguments were still going on, prompting additional fistfights, as late as November 14, when Billy Claiborne entered the Oriental and saw Leslie talking with a group of men. Claiborne assumed it was a discussion about the recent election, which it could have been, and shoved his way into the group. Here, in his own words, is Leslie's description of what happened next:

> I was talking with some friends in the Oriental Saloon when Claiborne came in and pushed his way in among us and began using very insulting language. I took him [to] one side and said, "Billy don't interfere, these people are friends among themselves, and are not talking about politics at all, and don't want you about." He appeared quite put out and used rather bad and certainly very nasty language towards me. I told him there was no use of him

fighting with me, and there was no occasion for it, and leaving him joined my friends.

He came back again and began using exceedingly abusive language, when I again took him by the collar of his coat and led him away, telling him not to get mad, that it was for his own good, that if he acted in that manner he was liable to get into trouble. He pushed away from me, using very harsh language, and as he started away shook his finger at me and said, "That's all right, Leslie, I'll get even on you," and went out of the saloon. In a short time a man came in and said there was a man waiting outside to shoot me, but I didn't pay much attention to it. A few minutes later another man came in looking quite white and said Claiborne was waiting outside with a rifle to shoot Frank Leslie.

I then went out, and as I stepped on the sidewalk saw about a foot of a rifle barrel protruding from the end of the fruit stand. I stepped out in the street and saw it was Claiborne, and said "Billy, don't shoot, I don't want you to kill me, and I don't want to have to shoot you." Almost before I finished he raised his gun and shot, and I returned the fire from my pistol, aiming at his breast. As soon as I shot I saw him double up and had my pistol cocked and aimed at him again when I saw, or thought I saw, another man by him, and I lowered the pistol, and when it was discharged the bullet went in the sidewalk.

After I fired, I advanced upon him, but did not shoot, when he said, "Don't shoot again; I am killed," which I didn't, but watched him, with my pistol at full cock, as I didn't know what game he might play to get me off my guard. At that moment officer [James] Coyle came up and took hold of my pistol hand. I told him to be careful, as it was at full cock. I then uncocked it and gave it to him, and said I would go with him. I told him I was sorry; that I might have done more, but I couldn't do less. He then placed me under arrest. [3]

On the day that Claiborne was killed, Leslie was supposed to have been out of town. He had made plans to take a trip to the Dragoon Mountains with George W. Parsons and others. That trip was cancelled because a horse that Parsons had bought from a rancher was not delivered to Tombstone on time. In his diary entry for that day, Parsons noted:

> Frank Leslie was to go with us and may yet, if he is not detained in the killing matter of this morning, and he ought not to be. He shot and killed the notorious Kid Claiborne this a.m. at 7:30, making as pretty a center shot on the Kid as one would wish to. The Kid threatened and laid for him near the Oriental with a Winchester, but Frank got the drop on him, being quick as lightning and used to killing men, and the Kid has gone to Hell. I say so because, if such a place exists and has bad men, he is there, as he was a notoriously bad egg and has innocent blood on his head. I state facts. Frank has done the country a service, and for that reason it is well that we did not get away sooner. Horse came today. If it had come yesterday or when expected, the Kid would have been alive. God almighty works in mysterious ways. I have contributed to the Kid's death. Frank didn't lose the light of his cigarette during the encounter. Wonderfully cool man.4

In his 1928 book, *Tombstone's Yesterday*, Lorenzo D. Walters offered a highly inaccurate motive for Claiborne's attempting to kill, as well as a description of the shooting that doesn't square with the known facts. According to Walters "Leslie went out of the back door, slipped around the side of the saloon to the front and located Billy Claiborne on the spot. Leslie did not ask him any questions but *shot him in the back*. [authors' italics] Claiborne lived long enough to declare that Leslie shot John Ringo by slipping up on him, *while he was in a drunken sleep*, and that he (Claiborne) was with him and saw him do it."[87] Walters doesn't make clear who Claiborne was "with" when Claiborne says that he "was with him and saw him do it." Was he "with" Leslie or Ringo? It really doesn't matter, since Walters's version is pure nonsense. The showdown between Leslie and Claiborne was the result of political animosity, caused by the race for sheriff. It had absolutely nothing to do with the death of John Ringo.

The inquest concluded with findings by the coroner's jury that Claiborne "came to his death from the effects of a pistol wound inflicted by Frank Leslie, in the town of Tombstone, Arizona Territory, on the 14th of November 1882, and that the shooting was done in self-defense, and, in the opinion of the jury was justifiable." [6]

At this point in his life the noted gunfighter had two known kills in stand-up gunfights where he could have been killed. Save for that simple twist of fate Michael D. Killeen or William "The Kid" Claiborne would have killed Buckskin Frank. Was it because he was so skilled in gun handling, or was it simply his good luck? If the latter, how long would his good luck hold out?

Chapter 8

The Magnolia Ranch

Late in 1882 Milton E. Joyce sold out his share in the Oriental Saloon, and took Leslie into partnership in a ranching venture near Arizona's Swisshelm Mountains. The Leslie-Joyce Ranch was called the "Magnolia" and was located nineteen miles from Tombstone in one of the most desolate stretches of southeastern Arizona. On November 9, 1882, a Los Angeles paper, under the heading of "Arizona Items," reported that "George Hearst has purchased the Mike Gray ranch at Cloverdale for $12,000. M. E. Joyce is the owner of the adjoining ranch."[1] George Hearst was a mining engineer and future United States senator. He was also the father of a first-year Harvard student named William Randolph Hearst.

On December 24, 1882, it was reported that "Frank Leslie of Tombstone met with a serious, and it is feared, fatal accident, a few evenings since. He was going home and had just turned the corner of Fifth and Safford streets, when he slipped, and he was precipited [*sic*] headfirst on a pile of rock, bruising and gashing his head in a frightful manner."[2] Leslie not only survived but recovered, but this was the second time he had suffered serious head injuries in less than three years. The previous occasion was on June 22, 1880, when two bullets fired by Mike Killeen had both grazed Leslie's head. This brutal fall may have been a contributing factor leading to severe mental issues (acknowledged by Leslie himself in an 1889 court document) that became progressively worse as the decade of the 1880s continued.

Milton E. Joyce had also been serving as Chairman of the Cochise County Board of Supervisors and had been charged with being less than honest in his job performance. At least one paper took a wait-and-see attitude on Joyce when it reported on February 18 that "the examination of M. E. Joyce, Chairman of the Board of Supervisors of Cochise County, shows fraud, but whether on the part of Joyce or some other party having access to the warrant book, which was kept insecurely, remains to be seen."[3]

Joyce, for his part, remained confident of his acquittal. On February 22 the same paper reported "M.E. Joyce, late chairman of the board of supervisors of Cochise County, arrived in town yesterday. . . . Legal troubles affect Mr. Joyce but slightly, and care finds no resting place on his placid brow. He is confident of a complete exoneration from the charges preferred against him, and declares he could be vindicated at once, but then he desires and insists upon a thorough investigation."[4]

While awaiting his "thorough investigation," Joyce got together with another celebrated resident of Tombstone. According to the *Arizona Daily Star*, "John H. Behan and M. E. Joyce, left for home this morning after spending a week in this city [Tucson] and taking in the races."[5] A Sacramento paper reported on the verdict of Joyce's trial on March 14, 1883, by saying "M. E. Joyce, who has been on trial for alleged crookedness during his term of office as Supervisor of the county, was today on motion of the Prosecuting Attorney, honorably acquitted, there being no evidence adduced that he had been guilty of the offense charged."[6]

Joyce left Leslie in charge of the ranch, so that he could concentrate on other business interests. Joyce's partner in those other interests was James Wilson Orndorff who would become a major figure in Leslie's final years. Orndorff was born in Ohio on April 7, 1834, and moved to California when he was eighteen. He prospected in the Yuba gold fields for nearly a decade before moving to Virginia City, Nevada, in 1863. In Virginia City he worked mining claims for the next seventeen years, eventually becoming the "overseer" of the Fairview Mine. Orndorff also ran the Ashland Hotel in Virginia City, as well as being in charge of the billiard rooms at the Washoe Hotel.

Orndorff enjoyed a reputation in Virginia City of being "second to none as an amateur billiardist." He got a chance to prove the claim in Truckee, California, on March 14, 1869, in a match against "the champion of the Pacific Coast." The *Truckee Tribune* reported that "a grand billiard match will take place at the Magnolia Theater tomorrow evening between James Orndorff of Virginia City, and E.W. Jameson, the champion of the Pacific coast. The latter will discount Orndorff, in a game of 500 points, for $250 a side."[7]

On September 27, 1875, Orndorff came close to being shot in Virginia City—by a woman. It was reported that "about 2 o'clock this afternoon a woman named Medley walked into the Delta Saloon, on C Street, and forcing her way through the crowd at the bar, drew out a pistol and attempted to shoot James W. Orndorff, one of the proprietors. Her arm was arrested by a bystander before she pulled the trigger, and she was given to the custody of a police officer. Jealousy is supposed to be the cause."[8]

The authors of an exhaustive study called *The History of the Comstock Lode 1850–1997* noted that "Jim Orndorff was the most prominent and successful saloonkeeper for years. Lived like a prince and kept a pack of hounds to hunt jack rabbits and coyotes, and deer in the Sierras in the fall."[9] Orndorff moved to San Francisco about 1880, where his proficiency at billiards led to his developing the "patent pool table," in which every ball dropped into a common box after passing the pocket. It was probably in San Francisco that Milton E. Joyce and James W. Orndorff first became acquainted.

After Joyce moved to Tombstone, Orndorff invested in both the Oriental and Magnolia Ranch holdings with Joyce. Except for a couple of trips to

Tombstone to look over his investments, Orndorff was content to remain in San Francisco as a silent partner. The Apaches were still a threat in the remote area where the Magnolia Ranch was located, as Leslie and a friend found out on March 25, 1883, when Capt. Charles Young and Frank had a fight with five Apaches. Leslie was surprised half a mile from camp but, after a running fight, succeeded in reaching the house where the two men held them off. All afternoon the Indians laid siege to the house, keeping up a steady fire from behind the surrounding rocks. They set fire to the grass in order to burn them out but the besiegers eventually gave up and left. Captain Young was positive that several were killed, but following their usual custom, they either buried the killed or carried them away.[10]

On April 1, 1883, a meeting was held in Tombstone calling for the organization of a militia force to deal with the Apache problem. At the meeting, Milton E. Joyce announced that he had a list of forty armed men who were ready to join such a militia force.[11] The "Tombstone Rangers" that were formed consisted of about sixty men, that were placed under the command of Captain Milton E. Joyce, who was turned down by Leslie when Joyce asked for his assistance. According to the *Arizona Daily Star*, "Capt. Joyce, of the Tombstone Rangers, sent a courier to Frank Leslie in the Swisshelm mountains the other day, requesting him to come and guide the outfit to the [San Carlos] reservation, but that he refused, saying that he was too busy, and that he did not think the command strong enough to make the attempt."[12]

Leslie knew what he was talking about. In his book *On the Border With Crook*, Capt. John G. Bourke explained why Leslie took such a dim view of the "Tombstone Rangers" when he recalled that the "men organized themselves into a company of military, remembered in the Territory as the 'Tombstone Toughs,' and marched upon the San Carlos [reservation] with the loudly heralded determination to 'clean out' all in sight. They represented all the rum-poisoned bummers of the San Pedro Valley, and no community was more earnest in the appeals to them to stay in the field until the last armed foe expired than was Tombstone, the town from which they had started; never before had Tombstone enjoyed such an era of peace and quiet, and the citizens appreciated the importance of keeping the 'Toughs' in the field as long as possible." The ridicule showered upon the Tombstone toughs did not continue with the comment upon the group's leader, Milton E. Joyce. He "was a much better man than the gang who staggered along on the trail behind him; he kept the best saloon in Tombstone, and was a candidate for political office."[13]

If Captain Bourke's account represented the military's view of the hapless Tombstone Rangers, the group fared even worse with an alarmed civilian front, as this account from the *Arizona Weekly Citizen* illustrated: "From time to time the rumor has reached this city [Tucson] that Captain Joyce, with his company of rangers, was going to San Carlos to attack the Indians on the reservation, and as often the rumor has been denied." That was a neutral comment. The following was definite praise for the man. "We have not the honor of Captain Joyce's acquaintance, and know nothing of the character of the man, but we hardly believe that he, with a handful of rangers, would openly make an attack on the reservation Indians, which could not result otherwise than in disaster to Captain Joyce and his command, and at this time would cause an outbreak of the reservation Indians which would result in the total annihilation of many settlements in southeastern Arizona."[14]

Leslie continued to keep as much distance as he could between himself and the Tombstone Rangers under the command of his business partner Milton E. Joyce and continued his work at the Magnolia Ranch. The *Santa Fe Daily New Mexican* reported that "Sunday [April 15, 1883] a Mexican lion was shot and killed by Frank Leslie and Frank Emmal at Joyce's Ranch in the Swisshelm Mountains of Arizona. It measured over six feet from tip to tip, and weighed about 100 pounds."[15]

On May 5, 1883, a Tucson paper reported that "Frank Leslie returned from his ranch in Sulphur Spring valley last night. He reports the country quiet, and entirely free from hostile Indians. Gen. Crook's pack train en route for the Sierra Madres, accompanied by about 400 troops, passed down the valley a few days since. The soldiers encamped in the vicinity of Joyce's ranch, in the Swisshelms, are kept busy scouting the surrounding country. They scout in small detachments and ride around the country for a distance of thirty or thirty-five miles every day, keeping a careful lookout for the approach of the Apaches."[16]

Leslie's ranching partner, Milton E. Joyce, was still playing a role in the Apache campaign, according to this May 19, 1883, report from a Tucson paper:

> Captain M.E. Joyce arrived last night from General Crook's headquarters near Guadalupe canyon. He brought the General's letters and dispatches, two of the latter being addressed to the Secretary of War in Washington. Major [James] Biddle is in command, the General having pushed forward to the interior of the Sierra Madres. His force in the field consists of 208 scouts, 50 soldiers under Captain [Adna] Chaffee, and 258 pack animals. Crook received the message from the Secretary of War before leaving headquarters. He tore it up and said he would go ahead until he had corralled the last renegade Apache, if he was cashiered for it. . . .
>
> Joyce's ranch is headquarters for two companies of soldiers, commanded by Captain Wallace. They are scouting from the Dragoons to the San Simon. . . . Captain Joyce made a ride of 85 miles yesterday [May 18, 1883] , in order to get the dispatches here within a specified time.[17]

Captain Milton E. Joyce's Tombstone Rangers had left a bad taste in many Arizona mouths by the time the group imploded in early June 1883. The newspapers rarely identified any of the sixty-man force by name. Captain Joyce was always identified by name and, as a result, was on the receiving end of all the vitriol that the fourth estate had to offer:

> The Tombstone Rangers seem to have subsided much sooner than might have been expected, considering their ferocious and sanguinary dispositions. Perhaps the fatigue attending their masterly retreat upon the San Carlos agency has cooled their ardor, or, more likely, the money which purchased their self-

> sacrificing patriotism has drowned them in a stream of liquid joy and pride, to wit —straight whiskey.
>
> It is reported that Captain Joyce has secretly purchased Harry Queen's Apache scalp, and now openly wears it on a shirt front in refutation of any and all slanders directed against his experience as a ranger soldier. Such a display is unnecessary. The soldier qualities of the Ranger Chieftain are fully appreciated by the public, as are the fighting qualities of the Apaches.
>
> The people of Arizona should certainly present Captain Joyce with some appropriate token of proper consideration for his late services in the field. Eight square inches of cactus, applied with vigorous and suggestive ceremonies to that part of him he most exposed to the foe, would be no more than he deserves. Such a public recognition would undoubtedly "tickle" the boss ranger, and satisfy even his enemies.[18]

On June 11, 1883, Leslie was hired as a dispatch rider and courier for the army. He made one round trip from the troops who were detached at Silver Creek, taking a message to Tombstone, and then returning to the troops. He had also carried a newspaper dispatch from a correspondent for the *El Paso Times*, who was with General Crook's troops. Leslie was paid $50 for his brief service.[19] Back at the Magnolia Ranch, Leslie and Joyce began to register their cattle brands. On June 20, 1883, the "M D" brand was registered, followed by the "7 UP" brand on June 25.[20] In time, the "7 UP" brand became so well known that the Magnolia Ranch was often referred to as being the "Seven-Up Ranch."

Not all of Leslie's encounters with Indians ended in violence. On August 7, 1883, a California newspaper described how several different groups of "friendly Apaches" met up with Leslie. According to the reporter "Frank Leslie, well known as 'Buckskin Frank,' a Government scout, stated to your reporter yesterday that he had met several small bands of Indians lately in the Chiricahuas, eleven in all, who were returning to the San Carlos reservation. They had made friendly advances, and he had talked with them."[21]

A Tucson paper reported on October 20, 1883, that "we are authorized by Frank Leslie, who has made thorough inquiries of the men who came in from his ranch . . . to state that there is little foundation for the Indian article that appeared in this morning's Epitaph. . . . The report of the killing of two men was told at the ranch by a Mormon, who heard it from another, who was told by another, who received it from another, and so on, that two men were killed near Willcox."[22] In early November 1883, a Phoenix newspaper printed an item, entitled "Surrender of the Indians," which detailed Leslie's latest stint as a scout for the Army:

> Tombstone, Nov. 2 – Buckskin Frank Leslie has just arrived from Camp Price, via Silver Creek. He reports eighty-two Indians at that place, twenty-three of whom are bucks. Among the squaws are those of the principal chiefs and warriors now out. Geronimo, with twenty-eight additional warriors, is expected in tomorrow. When he arrives, the command, consisting of two companies of cavalry as an escort, will depart with the hostiles to San Carlos.[23]

Apparently Geronimo didn't come in when expected. It wasn't until March 1, 1884, that the *Arizona Daily Star* reported that "Frank Leslie, who came in from the San Bernardino Ranch last evening, reports that Lieutenant Davis is now en route to the San Carlos reservation from Cloverdale with Geronimo, chief of the Chiricahuas, and thirty-seven Apaches." [24]

Between scouting engagements, Leslie usually returned to his Magnolia Ranch. On September 21, 1884, Leslie provided information for a document called *Great Register of the County of Cochise, Territory of Arizona, for the Year 1884*. This document was a list of registered voters for the county. His name appears as "Nashville Franklin [*sic*] Leslie," his age is given as forty-two, and his nativity as "United States." Leslie gave his occupation as "rancher," and his "Local Residence" as being the "Magnolia Ranch."[25]

The ranching venture was successful enough for Milton E. Joyce to leave Leslie in charge during 1884 in order to attend to his other business interests in San Francisco. When Joyce got back to San Francisco, he joined James W. Orndorff in opening the Baldwin Saloon and Billiard Parlor at the spectacular Baldwin Hotel built by Elias Jackson "Lucky" Baldwin. Joyce and Orndorff would remain there four years, until "Lucky" Baldwin decided he wanted the business for himself.

During December 1884, Leslie transferred his share of the "Mary Mine" to Lou Rickabaugh for ten dollars. Leslie and Rickabaugh had located the claim the previous year, and knew each other well from the Oriental Saloon, where Rickabaugh was in charge of the gambling rooms.[26]

Illustration 1. Nashville Franklyn "Buckskin Frank" Leslie (1842–1927)

(Drawing by Jack DeMattos)

Illustration 2. Frank Leslie's Arizona

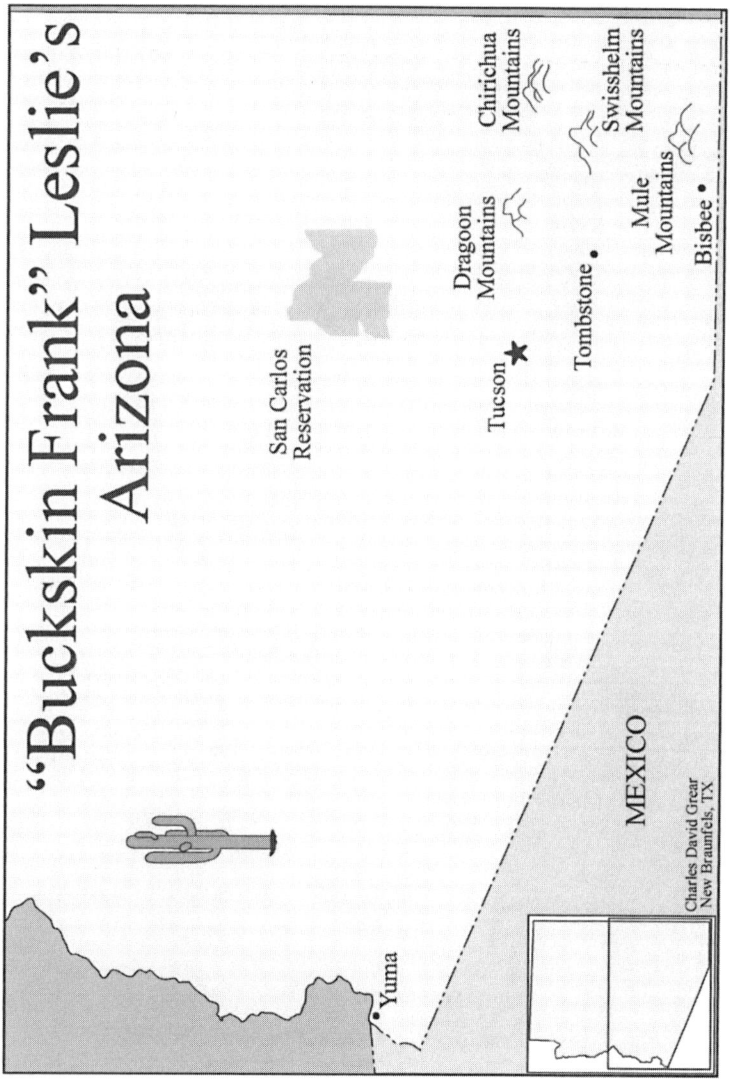

(Map by Charles David Grear)

Illustration 3. Tom Horn

(Drawing by Jack DeMattos)
Tom Horn (1860–1903) claimed in his autobiography that he, Leslie, and several others, were employed as scouts in Arizona during 1877. Historians dispute Horn's claim.

Illustration 4. Earliest likeness of Leslie.

(Courtesy Don Chaput)
This illustration is the earliest known likeness of Nashville Franklyn "Buckskin Frank" Leslie. It was published in the *Arizona Quarterly Illustrated* during July 1880. It shows Leslie at the age of thirty-eight, appropriately attired in a buckskin shirt.

Illustration 5. Albert Clay Bilicke

(Courtesy Don Chaput)
Bilicke (1861–1915), had just gone to bed at his family's hotel, when gunshots woke him up. Mary Killeen, the hotel's chambermaid, burst into his room screaming that her husband, Mike Killeen, had just shot Frank Leslie and was now coming to kill her. Nineteen-year-old Bilicke grabbed a pistol, which he wouldn't need, since Mike Killeen had already been mortally wounded. This photo of Albert Bilicke was taken more than thirty years later, not long before he became one of the victims on the torpedoed *Lusitania*.

Illustration 6. Mary Jane Evans

(Courtesy Epic Estate Auctions LLC)
Mary Jane Evans (1856–1947) married all three of her husbands in Tombstone within a nine-year period: Mike Killeen on April 13, 1880, followed by "Buckskin Frank" Leslie on July 6, 1880, and finally Alexander Durward on October 12, 1889. An original print of this photo (identified as "1880's Tombstone Prostitute Mary Killeen") was sold at auction on September 4, 2016. It should be noted that no evidence has been found suggesting that Mary Jane ever was, in fact, a prostitute.

Illustration 7. Leslie's belt buckle.

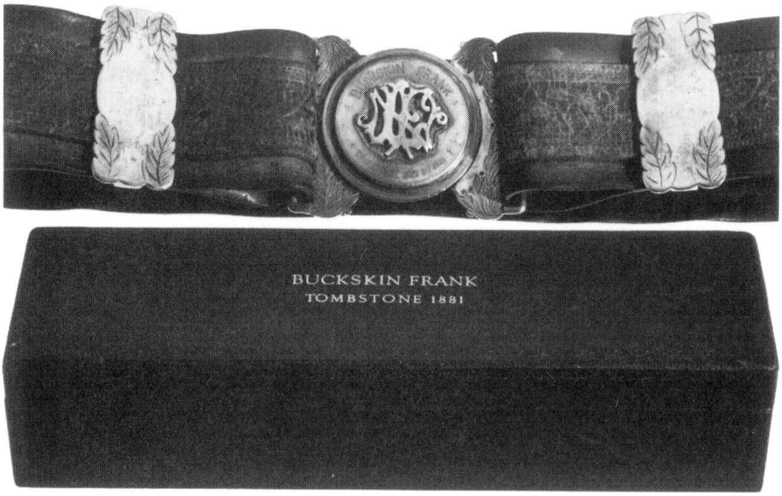

(Courtesy Heritage Auctions, Dallas, Texas)

During 1966 Western artifacts dealer Greg Martin discovered a gun belt with a massive 3.25-inch silver buckle that was inscribed "Buckskin Frank, Tombstone, Jan. 1, 1881." Fifty years after Greg Martin's initial discovery, the gun belt went up for auction at Heritage Auctions in Dallas on June 11, 2016. A collector successfully bid $26,000 for the gun belt—which was the highest amount paid for any item that went up for bid that day. This photo shows a portion of that gun belt, as well as the case (not contemporaneous to 1881) that came with it.

Illustration 8. Belt buckle close-up

(Courtesy Heritage Auctions, Dallas, Texas)
This is a close-up of the massive 3.25-inch silver belt buckle inscribed “Buckskin Frank” at the top and “Tombstone, Jan. 1, 1881” at the bottom. At the center is a design in which the letters “N,” “F,” and “L” (for Nashville Franklyn Leslie) are interlocked in an arrangement guaranteed to produce eyestrain.

Illustration 9. James Henry Tevis wearing Leslie's belt

(Courtesy Heritage Auctions, Dallas, Texas)

Included with the Leslie gun belt that went up for auction on June 11, 2016, was this photo of an "unidentified man" taken in 1886 by C.S. Fly at his Tombstone studio. The man shown here wears the same gun belt that had been inscribed to Leslie on Jan. 1, 1881. We now know that the man in this photo was James Henry Tevis (1837–1905) a notable figure in Arizona's history. Tevis and Leslie certainly knew each other in Tombstone—but the answer to the question of why Tevis happened to be wearing Leslie's gun belt when he posed for this photo, will probably never be known.

Illustration 10. Letter to Colt plant

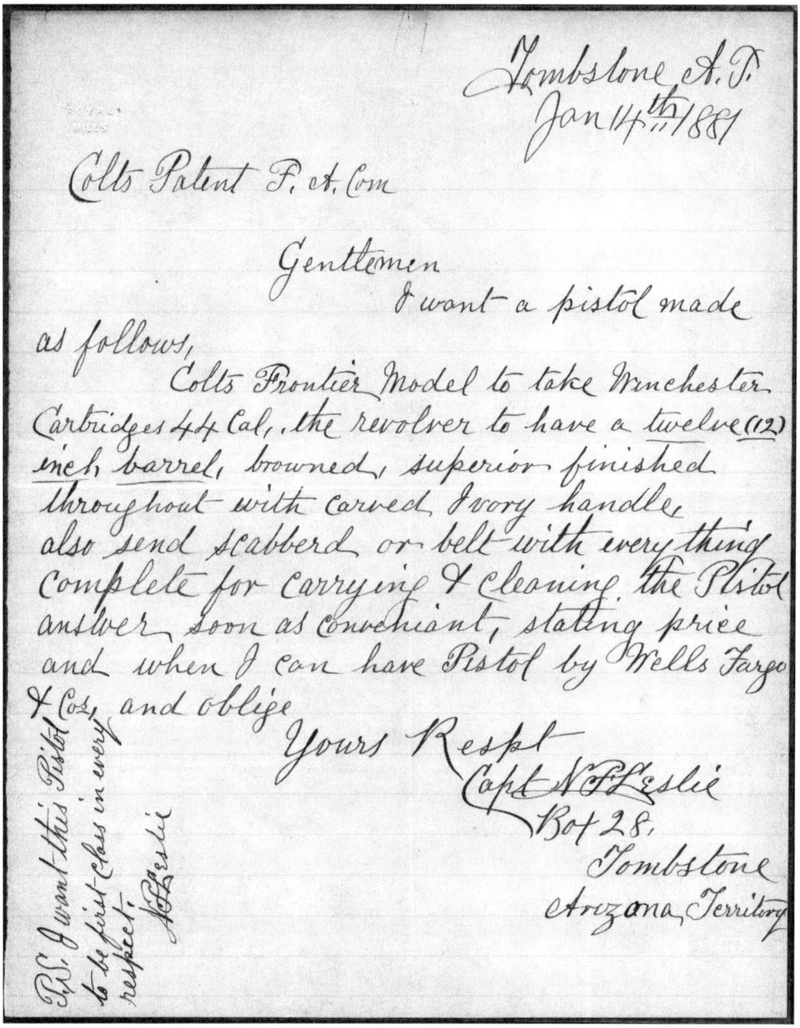

Tombstone A.T.
Jan 14th/1881

Colts Patent F. A. Com

Gentlemen

I want a pistol made as follows,

Colts Frontier Model to take Winchester Cartridges 44 Cal, the revolver to have a twelve (12) inch barrel, browned, superior finished throughout with carved Ivory handle also send scabberd or belt with every thing complete for carrying & cleaning the Pistol answer soon as Conveniant, stating price and when I can have Pistol by Wells Fargo & Cos, and oblige

Yours Respt

Capt N F Leslie
Box 28,
Tombstone
Arizona Territory

P.S. I want this Pistol to be first class in every respect. N F Leslie

(Courtesy Connecticut State Library, Hartford)

On January 14, 1881, "Buckskin Frank" —signing himself as "Capt. N.F. Leslie" —sent this letter to the Colt plant in Hartford, Connecticut, ordering a pistol with a "twelve inch barrel." Challenged for space, Leslie managed to squeeze in a postscript, written at a 90-degree angle (lower left) stating that "I want this pistol to be first class in every respect."

Illustration 11. John Peters Ringo

(Drawing by Jack DeMattos)
Ringo (1850–1882) was found shot in the head on July 14, 1882. His death was reported as being a "probable suicide," but many refused to accept that verdict insisting that Ringo had actually been killed by "Buckskin Frank" Leslie. Despite those claims, no one—including Leslie—would ever be officially charged with killing Ringo.

Illustration 12. William Milton "Billy" Breakenridge

(Courtesy Don Chaput)
Breakenridge (1846–1931) claimed that the story of Ringo being killed by Leslie had been promoted by Leslie himself. According to Breakenridge, Leslie claimed to have "met Ringo and had to kill him in self-defense, but the evidence proved this to be a lie. We all knew Leslie would not care to tackle him ..."

Illustration 13. Milton Edward Joyce

(Courtesy Gary L. Roberts)
Joyce (1847–1889) was a major figure in "Buckskin Frank" Leslie's life and in the history of Tombstone. He was one of the owners of the Oriental Saloon and partnered with Leslie in the Magnolia Ranch. Joyce is also remembered for a violent encounter that he had with Doc Holliday at the Oriental. Joyce, like Holliday, suffered from tuberculosis and died from the disease when he was only forty-two.

Illustration 14. William Floyd "Billy" Claiborne

(Courtesy Tombstone Epitaph)
William Floyd "Billy" Claiborne turned twenty-two shortly before being killed by "Buckskin Frank" Leslie in Tombstone on November 14, 1882.

Illustration 15. George Whitwell Parsons

(Courtesy Tombstone Epitaph)
George Whitwell Parsons (1850–1933) made diary entries during his Tombstone years that have provided an invaluable record of celebrated events as they happened. In his diary entry for the killing of Billy Claiborne by "Buckskin Frank" Leslie, Parsons wrote: "Frank didn't lose the light of his cigarette during the encounter. Wonderfully cool man."

Illustration 16. Plaque outside Oriental Saloon site

(Courtesy Dr. Judy Ohmer)
This plaque outside the building that housed Tombstone's Oriental Saloon marks the location of two of the town's celebrated gunfights.

Illustration 17. Newly discovered photo of Leslie

(Courtesy Robert G. McCubbin)

The noted Old West photograph collector Robert G. McCubbin thought the man in this photo looked a lot like Leslie, but lacked solid provenance to verify that it was him. The authors of this book decided to conduct a test by having Leslie's head in his authenticated 1893 prison photo, and the man's head in this photo blown up to an identical size and printed on clear acetate. When this image was placed over the 1893 image, the distance between the eyes, the shape of the ears and nose and even the hairline all lined up exactly, convincing the authors that this is indeed a photo of "Buckskin Frank" Leslie.

Illustration 18. C.S. Fly photograph of Geronimo

(Courtesy Western History Collections, University of Oklahoma Libraries, N.H. Rose Collection, Image No. 855)

Tombstone photographer C.S. Fly took this photo of Geronimo meeting with General George Crook in Sonora, Mexico, on March 27, 1886. Geronimo is seated on the left. General Crook is on the right wearing a pith helmet. Capt. John G. Bourke, the author of the 1891 classic *On the Border With Crook*, is the man seated next to the general.

Illustration 19. Birdie Woods

(Courtesy J. Levine Auction & Appraisal LLC, Scottsdale, Arizona)
Birdie Woods was accused of having "illicit relations" with "Buckskin Frank" between July 4–6, 1886, when Mary Jane "May" Leslie decided to institute divorce proceedings. The original of this photo was sold at auction on July 9, 2015. The photo was described as being that of a "Tombstone prostitute" named Birdie Woods. Extant newspaper accounts record Birdie Woods as actually being another sort of entertainer—a singer.

Illustration 20. *Harper's Weekly's* "The Scout"

(Courtesy Don Chaput)

Harper's Weekly published an illustration by Rufus Fairchild Zogbaum (1849–1925) called "The Scout" on the cover of their issue for August 11, 1888. While the scout in Zogbaum's drawing wears buckskins, it was not meant to portray "Buckskin Frank" Leslie. Nonetheless, it does give us an idea of how Leslie *might* have looked during his service as a scout in the Apache campaign.

Illustration 21. Mollie Edwards's grave

(Jack DeMattos Collection)
Mollie Edwards was killed by "Buckskin Frank" Leslie on July 10, 1889, and was buried within sight of his Magnolia Ranch. This photo, taken on June 16, 1980, shows co-author Jack DeMattos standing next to Mollie Edwards's grave. In the distance are Arizona's Swisshelm Mountains.

Illustration 22. Marker on Mollie Edwards's grave

(Jack DeMattos Collection)

On August 20, 1970, this marker was placed over Mollie Edwards's grave —which previously had been marked only by a pile of rocks. The problem with the belated "Gone But Not Forgotten" epitaph is that two significant details clearly had been forgotten. Mollie's correct surname was Edwards, not Williams, and she was killed on July 10, 1889, not July 11.

Illustration 23. Sheriff John Horton Slaughter

(Drawing by Jack DeMattos)

Sheriff Slaughter (1841–1922) delivered "Buckskin Frank" Leslie to Yuma Territorial Prison where Leslie was logged in as convict No. 632 on January 10, 1890.

Illustration 24. Yuma Territorial Prison

(Courtesy Don Chaput)
The Yuma Territorial Prison opened in 1875 and closed in 1909. This was how It looked in the 1890s, when "Buckskin Frank" Leslie was an inmate.

Illustration 25. Enoch Austin Shattuck

(Courtesy Don Chaput)
Enoch Austin Shattuck (1848–1911) served as John Horton Slaughter's Undersheriff. He was also the administrator of the late Milton E. Joyce's Arizona estate —which included the Magnolia Ranch, which Leslie also held an interest in. Soon after entering the Yuma Territorial Prison as Convict No. 632, Leslie signed over his share of the Magnolia Ranch to Shattuck for $10.

Illustration 26. "Buckskin Frank" Leslie's most reproduced likeness

(Courtesy Don Chaput)
This is "Buckskin Frank" Leslie's most reproduced likeness. It was taken at the Yuma Territorial Prison on or about November 30, 1893. It was not—strictly speaking—a prison "mug shot." It had been taken at the specific request of a *San Francisco Chronicle* reporter named W.H. Cameron, who had just interviewed Leslie. The photo formed the basis for a line drawing that was published with Cameron's article on December 3, 1893.

Illustration 27. Leslie's 1893 prison photo, retouched.

(Jack DeMattos Collection)

This could pass as a "high definition" print of Leslie's 1893 prison photo, but it is actually a retouched photo used for a *Real West* article in 1965. Co-author Jack DeMattos found it while he served on the staff of the magazine from 1979 to 1988. It was salvaged from a stack of retouched photos about to be thrown out. In this image, Leslie's hair and mustache are examples of photo retouching at its best. Less successful are the odd-looking eyeballs and ear on the left side of the photo—both created from scratch by the retouching artist. The imagined ear ended up being slightly smaller than Leslie's actual ear on the right side. In the original 1893 prison photo only one ear was visible, while the other was obscured by deep shadow.

Illustration 28. *San Francisco Chronicle* drawing of Leslie

(Jack DeMattos Collection)
The *San Francisco Chronicle* published this line drawing of Leslie on Saturday, December 3, 1893, stating that it was drawn "from a photograph taken a few days ago at the Arizona Territorial Prison."

Illustration 29. General Henry Ware Lawton

(Courtesy Arizona Historical Society. No. 73368)
General Henry Ware Lawton (1843–1899) was highly regarded by his former scout, "Buckskin Frank" Leslie. Lawton's death in the Philippines on December 19, 1899, inspired Leslie to compose a lengthy tale of their experiences in the Apache Wars of the 1880s. Leslie's account was published as a full-page illustrated article in the *San Francisco Call* on January 7, 1900.

Illustration 30. Leslie's "Personal Experiences With the late General Lawton"

THE SUNDAY CALL. 5

Personal Experiences With the Late General Lawton

Told by Captain N. Frank Leslie. His Chief of Scouts in the Apache Campaign.

(Jack DeMattos Collection)

Leslie's heavily illustrated article "Personal Experiences With the Late General Lawton" filled all of page 5 in the Sunday, January 7, 1900, issue of the *San Francisco Call*. This is a detail which shows the top half of that page, along with some of the illustrations. The author's byline was "Captain N. Frank Leslie." He further identified himself as General Lawton's "Chief of Scouts in the Apache Campaign." The entire text of Leslie's *San Francisco Call* article can be found in Appendix C of this book.

Illustration 31. James Wilson Orndorff

(Jack DeMattos Collection)
Orndorff (1834–1923) was major figure in "Buckskin Frank" Leslie's life, particularly during his final years. This image of Orndorff is from an 1893 book called *Hunting for Gold* by Major William Downie.

Illustration 32. Elnora Torbert Cast

(Courtesy Cathie S. Grant, Elnora's great grand-daughter)
Elnora Torbert Cast (1868–1932) became the last (known) wife of "Buckskin Frank" Leslie when she married him on November 6, 1913.

Illustration 33. Leslie in his seventies.

(Courtesy David E. Dean III Collection)
Published here for the first time is a photo of Buckskin Frank Leslie when he was in his seventies. It was taken in Washington State, sometime between 1913 and 1920 by his longtime friend John Ralph Dean. By this period of his life Leslie no longer sported his sweeping mustache, but he still managed to take his famous buckskin jacket out of mothballs for the purposes of this photo. The back of the photo was inscribed "Nashville Frank Leslie" by John Ralph Dean and is now part of a collection owned by Dean's great-grandson.

Chapter 9

Government Scout in the Apache Campaign

Leslie's peaceful interlude at the Magnolia Ranch ended when several Apaches, led by Geronimo, bolted from the reservation. On May 20, 1885, Leslie and Andrew Ames enlisted as scouts for Troops B, D, and I of the Fourth Cavalry under Captain Henry Ware Lawton. They would be operating out of Guadalupe Canyon.[1] Leslie's return to Tombstone on June 16, was detailed in this report, which identified Leslie not only as a scout, but a "sharp shooter" as well:

> Frank Leslie, better known as "Buckskin Frank," a sharp shooter and scout returned this morning from Sonora. He has been acting as a scout for [Henry Ware] Lawton's command, consisting of three companies, under Lawton, Wood and Hatfield. This regiment is the same that was reported some days since as charging a band of Indians down the east side of the Chiricahuas into the Sierra Madres. The Indians pursued are the band who killed the five soldiers and destroyed the baggage wagons in Guadalupe canyon.
>
> The trail was a large one and led through a country impassable for horses. The soldiers were compelled to walk nearly the whole

> distance. The regiment penetrated into Mexico as far south as Bavispe. The Indians camped in inaccessible places, choosing high elevations from which they could command the country for miles around. The trail of the Indians was strewn with dead horses that succumbed to exhaustion and lack of feed, attendant to their hasty flight. Lawton followed until his horses gave out, and further progress was impossible.
>
> Leslie says the troops climbed the most impassable gorges and mountain heights, and every effort that human exertion could put forth, was made by the troops to overtake the flying Apaches, but to no avail, inasmuch as the Indians sacrificed animals ruthlessly to expedite their march, while the troops were necessarily obliged to preserve their horses. On their return they found a Mexican ranch, forty miles below San Bernadino ranch, burned and plundered, but not apparently the work of Indians, as no signs were apparent in the neighborhood. Leslie, who brings the news, has ridden 148 miles today, and leaves on horseback at one a.m., tomorrow for Huachuca, with military dispatches.[2]

Leslie served as a scout until June 21, and returned to his Magnolia Ranch. He didn't remain at the ranch long, and was soon back in the field serving with Captain Wirt Davis as chief of scouts.[3] The *Arizona Daily Star* reported that "Frank Leslie who is now acting as chief of scouts under Gen. Crook, is in the Sierra Madre mountains with 100 Indian scouts. He has not been heard from since he crossed the line into Sonora on the 10th of July." [4]

In the meantime, Milton E. Joyce was back in California where he demonstrated that going to the seashore wasn't always "a day at the beach." According to an account published in a local paper, "Capt. M. E. Joyce created his annual sensation on the beach Saturday [July 11, 1885] morning by appearing in a striped suit, and playing tag with the breakers. Joyce may not be afraid of the Apaches, but a big breaker makes him run every time."[5]

Leslie left the day-to-day operation of the ranch to twenty-one-year-old John Ralph "Johnny" Dean who was soon to become a major figure in Leslie's life. On July 31, 1885, the *Daily Tombstone* reported that "John R. Dean came in last night from the Patton and Leslie ranch, where he is stopping during the absence of Frank Leslie, who is now in the Sierra Madre."[6] On August 17 Dean made another visit to Tombstone where he mistakenly gave Captain Wirt Davis a promotion to Major in this update he gave to a reporter:

> John Dean arrived in Tombstone from the Swisshelms, last evening. He states that Frank Leslie, who has been acting as chief of scouts under Major Davis' command, now operating against the renegade Apaches in the Chihuahua, arrived at the ranch last night in company with a couple of Mexicans. Leslie left Davis' command about a week ago, and is the bearer of dispatches from Major Davis to General Crook at Fort Bowie.
>
> He states that a day or two before his departure the scouts struck a band of the hostiles about 250 miles south of the line numbering about twenty-five, and after a sharp conflict, the hostiles fled, leaving eight of their number dead on the field. Among those slain was Nana, a prominent Chiricahua chief. In addition to the Indians killed, there were about fifteen squaws, and children captured. It is also known that a number of the renegades were wounded.
>
> Quite a number of horses and mules, which had been stolen from the Mexicans were recovered. Leslie, it is learned, reports that with the exception of the squaws and children no prisoners were taken.
>
> Previous reports about Chato having mutinied and been killed are without foundation. Among the eight good Indians now in Chihuahua, is a twelve or thirteen year old boy whom the captured squaws say is a son of Geronimo. The squaws also say that the noted Apache chief was wounded.7

In his official report, General Crook noted that "Mr. Leslie, who brought in Captain Davis's report, states that he swam the Bavispe River eleven times in one day, a stream that is usually easily forded. It should be understood that the Indians are so split up in small parties and are so constantly on the watch that our scouts are practically compelled to cover the entire region."[8] The *Arizona Daily Star* printed a dispatch headlined "Decisive Battle" which read, "Bowie, Aug. 17. —Scout Leslie has just arrived in camp and reports that the command of Major [*sic*] Davis met a party of Indians on the 7th instant and killed Chief Nana and seven others. He also captured eighteen squaws. Geronimo and one buck got away from the party. Geronimo was badly wounded. The fight occurred 200 miles south of the line." [9]

This concluded Leslie's scouting activities for the moment, and he returned to the Magnolia Ranch. During October, Leslie submitted a further claim of $165 from the government for service he performed serving Captain Henry Ware Lawton. Leslie's payment was approved.[10]

A certain "Judge Berry" put his own life at risk, on a Tombstone street, when he decided to abuse Leslie's dog during October 1885. According to the *Daily Tombstone* "one of Judge Berry's latest achievements is breaking the jaw and otherwise injuring a dog belonging to Frank Leslie, simply because the dog was fighting. There should be a cruelty to animal society here for the benefit of such brutes as he is."[11]

Leslie was once again hired to perform scouting duties early in 1886. The *Tombstone Daily Epitaph* gave this report:

> Frank Leslie, the government scout, well known in this section as "Buckskin Frank," came in yesterday [January 13,1886] evening from Capt. Crawford's command, sixteen miles south of Nacosari, a small town above Sahuaripa, Sonora. Crawford had discovered no hostile trails up to the time of Leslie's departure on Jan. 4. On Leslie's return, when passing Mud Springs, in this country, two couriers, belonging to the Tenth cavalry, a colored regiment, reported that there had been some trouble between an Indian agent and a quartermaster at Cave Creek, Capt. Kennedy's station, twenty

> five miles south of Bowie, on the east Slope of the Chiricahua mountains.
>
> The misunderstanding arose from a complaint on the part of the Apache scout about the quantity of the bread issued. After some hard words had passed between the quartermaster and the Indian scout, the latter went to his camp, returned with his rifle, shot the quartermaster and the quartermaster's sergeant dead and fled. The officer in charge commanded his men, who were about to fire upon the offender, to spare his life, as he wished to take him alive. The result was, as usual, that the murderer escaped, thus adding one more to the forces of the hostiles and an especially vindictive one, well supplied with information as to the position and number of all troops and scouts in the field.[12]

Leslie had left the command of Captain Emmett Crawford, in Mexico, on January 4 and arrived in Tombstone on January 13. While Leslie was en route to Tombstone, Crawford was shot in the head by a Mexican Irregular on January 10. An Apache scout pulled the mortally wounded Crawford to safety and then killed the Mexican soldier who had shot him. Crawford did not die immediately, and lingered until January 18.

The news of Crawford's death took more than a week to reach Tombstone. When it did, a reporter "called on Mr. Frank Leslie, well-known as 'Buckskin Frank,' and learned from him that nothing could have been heard from Captain Crawford's command save by special courier from that camp as it would be a physical impossibility for anyone to have gone there and returned since his last report. Upon his last return he gave the particulars of the killing of the quartermaster and sergeant by a rebellious Apache scout. The death of Captain Crawford as reported . . . at Fort Bowie was sorrowful intelligence to Mr. Leslie as well as to the rest of this community."[13]

Two famous former residents of Tombstone were in Los Angeles giving testimony at a trial. On February 14, 1886, the *Epitaph* reported that "M. E. Joyce and Vergil [*sic*] Earp, are witnesses in the famous Baldwin divorce case which is now in progress in Los Angeles."[14] Two weeks later, Joyce and his wife became parents. According to the *Daily Epitaph*, "the *San Francisco Call* contains the following: 'JOYCE —In the city, February 28, to the wife of M. E. Joyce, a son.' Here's to our Milton, old boy. Better late than never." [15] Back in Arizona, Leslie was between scouting engagements and decided to seek employment as a Mounted Customs Inspector by submitting this application for employment:

Tombstone, Arizona
March 10, 1886

Hon. Joseph Magoffin
Collector of Customs
El Paso, Texas

Sir

I hereby submit this my application for appointment for the position of Mounted Inspector for the Port of [illegible] Arizona. I, Nashville Franklyn Leslie, was born near San Antonio Texas on the 18th day of March 1842 and am now a resident of Tombstone Arizona, and have been a resident of Arizona for nine years. I have a good common school education. Present occupation rancher. I never was employed in the Navy but was connected with the Army as Chief of Scouts, Courier and Guide during several Indian Campaigns and was honorably discharged with the expiration of term of Service.

I hereby certify on honor that this application has been written and composed without assistance and that these statements contained herein are true, that I am a citizen of the United States, and faithful to the Union and Constitution.

N.F. LESLIE[16]

This letter is the second time that Leslie gave Texas as his birth place on an official document. Previously, on June 3, 1880, Leslie had told a United States Federal Census enumerator that he had been born in Texas. The information he gave in his application for employment was far more specific when he said that he was "born *near* San Antonio." Leslie did not say he was born in San Antonio itself, but someplace "near" it which, at the time of his 1842 birth, would have included numerous large and small settlements, as well as isolated farms.

The exploits of the man known as "Buckskin Frank" were frequently reported in various California newspapers. His name turned up often enough to inspire the *San Jose Evening News* to publish some verse, entitled "Buckskin Frank," that threatened to give doggerel a bad name. Altogether it contained seven stanzas of which this will have to suffice:

> Told an Eastern crank
>
> He was Buckskin Frank.
>
> That with scalps his valise was filled;
>
> Thirteen years a scout
>
> And always made out
>
> To get away without getting killed.[17]

Only ten days after sending his 1886 letter of application, Leslie was in the saddle as a U.S. Mounted Custom Inspector, along with a partner named Tom Green. The *Epitaph* gave this report of a shooting involving Green and some Mexicans:

> Last Saturday [March 20, 1886] Messrs. Frank Leslie and Tom Green, mounted U.S. Custom Inspectors, reached La Noria in search of some smugglers. While resting quietly, some Mexicans came up to Mr. Green and without any provocation began to abuse him. When Green mounted his horse and rode across the line the Mexicans began firing at him. When on American soil, Mr. Green turned and fired at the Mexicans and it is thought wounding one

> of them. One of the shots from the Mexicans grazed Mr. Green's neck and another passed through his coat.[18]

The *Epitaph* offered no information on where Leslie was when the shots were being fired by Green and the Mexicans. Somehow Leslie managed to perform double duty as a Government scout for General George Crook while also serving as a Mounted Customs Inspector. General Crook kept a daily journal, and two of his entries from March 1886 refer to Leslie:

> MARCH 28. Left camp early in the morning for San Bernardino. Met Geronimo and Norche [Naiche?] and other Chiricahuas coming from the San Bernardino direction quite drunk. We took buck-board at San Bernadino and took lunch at Silver Creek with Capt. Smith. Stopped A moment at Lt Wheeler's camp at Mud Springs, and stopped for the night at Frank Leslie's ranch.
>
> MARCH 29. Left Leslie's at six A.M. Wind blew a gale all day. Arrived at Fort Bowie at about 3 P.M. Killed a curlew [a bird], the Largest I ever saw in Sulphur Springs Valley.[19]

Leslie still managed to get some work done as a Mounted Customs Inspector. According to the *Tombstone Daily Epitaph* "Frank Leslie, who is now a mounted inspector on the line, came in from Bisbee yesterday [April 3, 1886] with two Mexican smugglers."[20] A glowing report of this April 3, 1886, appearance in Tombstone by Leslie was also given by the *San Francisco Chronicle*:

> The celebrated scout, Frank Leslie, known as Buckskin Frank, at present a mounted Inspector of Customs, arrived here this evening. Mr. Leslie was for many years Chief of Scouts, and is in the confidence of General Crook, and is personally acquainted with Geronimo and the other leading chiefs. He has just arrived from the camp of the hostile prisoners, at White's ranch. He had a long conversation with the hostiles who have been on the warpath all summer; also with General Crook and staff. From him came the following true version of the cause of Geronimo's departure after the surrender was obtained.

> Geronimo, Natchez and Chihuahua at the conference, after some talk, unconditionally surrendered. While Crook was on his way back from the conference, and half way from that place to the line, all the Indians got very drunk and were ready for a fight. There was shooting in all directions, and the Indians had set fire to the grass in several directions. Leslie saw Crook at San Bernardino, and Crook remarked that liquor might prevent the Indians from coming in, and it would be a wonder if they came in at all.
>
> Subsequently Leslie learned from Chihuahua, Nana, Dutchy and the squaws that Geronimo, Natchez and the band were beastly intoxicated at the time of the desertion, and much liquor was in their possession at that time. Chihuahua intimated that after the effects of whisky had worked off the Indians might repent their action and return. Mr. Leslie thinks this also, as do other Indians. Leslie says Natchez is hereditary chief of the Chiricahuas, but Geronimo assumed the position owing to greater brain power, Natchez lacking force of character. The Indians call Geronimo a second Napoleon. [21]

Given the typical 1886 Apache's absolute lack of familiarity with the first Napoleon, the authors feel safe in describing the final sentence of this article as hyperbole. The *San Francisco Chronicle* account infuriated Charles Fletcher Lummis, the city editor of the *Los Angeles Times,* who had recently met Leslie in Arizona. The response from Lummis came in the form of this blistering broadside, headlined "Scouts and Liars."

> This man Leslie is a peculiar case—one of the types of a class not infrequently met on the frontier. A man apparently well educated, gentlemanly and liked by all who know him; with as much "sand" as the country he ranges—but [also is] a novelist who can make a little truth go as far as any one in the Territory. As much fact as you could pick up on a pin point would last him a year. But there is one thing about it, his prevarications are all harmless. He never lies to hurt anybody—and least of all to hurt Frank Leslie.

> It is the prime ambition of his existence to figure as a scout—and a scout he will be, if wild-cat dispatches from Tombstone can make him one. He was for a few weeks connected with Capt. Crawford's command, hunting Geronimo, but was directly discharged because of his inability to tell a trail from a box of flea powder. Therein lies his claim to distinction as a celebrated scout. But though no scout, he is no dude. He has killed two men, under circumstances of Arizona propriety, is a fine shot, and can ride farther and harder in a day than any other white man you can rake up with a fine toothed comb. As to his "enjoying Gen. Crook's confidence," I guess it isn't necessary to say anything—but you ought to have heard the quiet old General laugh when I showed him that dispatch. Well, so much for that sort of news fodder. [22]

Lummis later added insult to injury when he wrote about the complaints of some of Crook's white scouts about the Apache scouts. Lummis wrote that "the howl against the Apache scouts came largely from alleged white scouts of the Frank Leslie stamp, who want the position for themselves. The real white scouts, men like Al Seeber [*sic*] . . . cheerfully admit that Apache scouts are indispensible."[23] Leslie found himself cast in an unusual role on April 24, 1886, when according to the *Epitaph* "the Greco-Roman wrestling match at Schieffelin Hall on Saturday evening last between Greek George and Pete Schumacher, resulted in a victory for the latter. Mr. Ed Wilson, a well known local athlete, officiated as referee, and Messrs. Frank Leslie and G.S. Bradshaw, as time keepers. A large crowd was in attendance."[24]

John O. Dunbar, who owned a share of the *Epitaph*, as well as part of a business called the Fashion Stables, was having legal troubles as a result of a suit brought by Leslie. A rival newspaper, the *Daily Tombstone*, undoubtedly took some pleasure in reporting that "the sale of J.O. Dunbar's interest in the Epitaph, to satisfy an execution in favor of Frank Leslie, which was advertised for today, has been postponed until May 17th." [25] The case was actually resolved on May 16, when Leslie was awarded a judgment against Dunbar following a "Sheriff's Sale." The

Daily Tombstone reported that "Sheriff Hatch sold this morning to satisfy an execution in favor of Frank Leslie for between six and seven hundred dollars, all of J.O. Dunbar's interest in the horses and rolling stock of the Fashion stables."[26]

The day after Leslie won his judgment against John O. Dunbar, the next woman whom he would be involved with arrived in Tombstone. Her arrival was hyped by the *Daily Tombstone* that reported "the Crystal Palace Saloon has secured the services of Miss Birdie Woods of San Francisco, who will make her first appearance this evening as a vocal and instrumental musician."[27] The singer was a hit and got a rave review that said "Miss Birdie Woods made her debut at the Crystal Palace last evening and made a decidedly favorable impression."[28] There was no doubt about the "favorable impression" Birdie Woods made on Frank Leslie. Within six weeks they would be an item.

The Indian campaign remained headline news. The *Daily Tombstone* reported that "from Johnny Dean who arrived from the Swisshelms today [May 18, 1886] it is learned that Lieut. Wheeler with Troop E of the Fourth Cavalry, passed Leslie's ranch yesterday morning en route from Fort Rucker to join Captain Hatfield's command."[29] Troop E was headed across the border in the direction of Cananea, Sonora, Mexico —an area that Leslie knew well.

During June, the *Daily Epitaph* reported that "Frank Leslie came in from the line, yesterday [June 9, 1886]. He says on the day before, seven hostiles passed within a few yards of Green's ranch, on the San Pedro, where Mr. Green has his family."[30] For four days the following month —from July 3 to July 6—Leslie would move into "Miss" Birdie Wood's residence on Fremont Street. The fact that she actually was *Mrs.* Birdie Woods, didn't concern Leslie in the least. This wasn't his first experience with a married woman. It was convenient for both of them that Birdie's husband, Dick Woods, was out of town, and May Leslie was at the ranch. Since neither Birdie or Leslie were models of discretion, it didn't take long before the spouses learned of their affair.

Within a few days of his liaison with Birdie Woods, a reporter from the *Tombstone Democrat* said, "Frank Leslie came in from his Swisshelm ranch Thursday [July 8]. He reports a great many depredations from horse thieves in that vicinity. Eleven head have been taken from his ranch alone."[31]

On July 13, 1886, Leslie sent a letter of resignation ending his brief career as a Mounted Custom Inspector.[32] As far as can be determined, Leslie appears to have spent the remaining months of 1886 at his Magnolia Ranch. The *Epitaph* printed one of his final press notices for the year when it reported that "Frank Leslie came in yesterday [September 10, 1886] from his ranch in the Swisshelms. He reports the grass as splendid and the stock in fine condition."[33]

Chapter 10

Lady Killer

John Ralph Dean was born in Carson City, Nevada, on November 28, 1863. He was more than twenty-one years younger than Leslie, but would remain, off and on, part of Leslie's life into the 1920s. Dean would later claim to have been involved with Leslie at the Magnolia Ranch as an equal partner, but the evidence shows that he was employed as a foreman. Dean also claimed active involvement in the Apache Campaign. Perhaps he did participate, but his claim is tempered by Dean's other boasts such as riding for the Pony Express (which ceased to exist before Dean was born) and serving as a Texas Ranger. The youthful Dean was in charge of running the Magnolia Ranch when Leslie was away—which was the majority of the time. On January 1, 1887, Leslie was a guest at the wedding of the twenty-three-year-old Dean to nineteen-year-old Katie Quadlin. The witnesses were Mrs. May Leslie and Mrs. Josephine Eccleston, the bride's aunt.[1]

In the decades that followed, in Arizona, Texas, California, and possibly elsewhere, Dean and Leslie would often reconnect after gaps that spanned several years. As a young man in Tombstone, Dean was called "Johnny." As he grew older, he changed that to "Jack" —with a military rank, such as "Captain" or "Colonel" often preceding the "Jack." Dean never met a reporter he didn't like and gave many interviews over the years in which he never failed to mention Leslie. His obsession with Leslie reached its apex during an 1892 Chicago interview, when he identified himself as being "Buckskin Jack" Dean.[2] While some of Dean's many claims may be true, there is always the thought that he had elected to "remember with advantages." [3]

"Frank Leslie is in from his Magnolia ranch and reports an abundance of snow, slush and mud, and a total absence of summer." So reported the *Tombstone Daily Epitaph* during early February 1887.[4] On March 9 the same paper reported that "Frank Leslie will take his departure in a few days for San Carlos, to assume command of the Indian police at that place. Frank is one of the most fearless scouts in the service, and will fill the position with ability and credit; moreover, he will make the young Geronimo's [*sic*] toe the mark."[5] The *Tombstone Democrat* also endorsed Leslie's appointment saying that "Frank Leslie has been appointed chief of scouts of the San Carlos Indian Agency, and will assume his duties as such in a few days. Frank is well known as a brave and daring scout, and will always be found ready to do his duty." [6]

Milton E. Joyce was the principal partner, along with J.J. Patton and Frank Leslie, in their ranching venture in the Swisshelm Mountains. On March 22, 1887, under the headline "A Ranch Sale," it was reported that Joyce was buying out one of his partners:

> M. E. Joyce arrived in Tombstone recently for the purpose of inspecting his ranch and cattle, which is located in the Swisshelm Mountains. Mr. Joyce had two partners in the business, Messrs. J.J. Patton and Frank Leslie. After visiting he concluded to purchase the interest of Mr. Patton, and a bargain was made on the spot, Joyce paying Patton $3,000 for his interest. Mr. Joyce, who is a very successful business man, will place at once on the place 400 additional cows, which will place him up among the heavy cattle men of Cochise County. This country is rapidly coming to the front as the leading cattle country of Arizona, and its claims are based upon the fact long since established that it has more acres

> of valleys and mesa grass than any other section of our Territory. Our winters are mild and the water supply is abundant, all of which tends to make Cochise County the leading cattle county of Arizona.[7]

Back in California it was reported on May 10, that the Magnolia Ranch had acquired, in Joyce's opinion, an interesting new feature. According to the report, "Colonel M. E. Joyce of the Baldwin hotel bar and billiard rooms, is inclined to think that the volcano which is reported to have broken forth in Arizona is on his property and is, consequently, congratulating himself on owning one of the first-class attractions of the continent. Should the volcano prove to be a genuine article the Colonel will at once erect a hotel close to it for the accommodation of tourists." [8]

Mary Jane "May" Leslie filed for divorce on May 27, 1887. In her complaint, May charged that "on the third, fourth, fifth and sixth days of July A.D. 1886 at the house of one Mrs. Woods, situated on the north side of Fremont Street, near Sixth Street at the City of Tombstone, defendant committed adultery with one Birdie Woods." May also charged that Leslie had choked and beaten her on March 9, 1887. The divorce was granted on June 3, 1887, by Judge William H. Barnes. She was awarded a $650 cash settlement. Judge Barnes also ruled that Leslie had to convey title to a one-fourth interest in the Magnolia Ranch, which included thirteen horses and 150 head of cattle. Leslie was also ordered to pay all legal fees in the case.[9]

This is an appropriate place to address the myth of Leslie standing his wife against a wall and outlining her figure with bullets. The many accounts claiming this story to be true usually describe May Leslie as being known as the "Silhouette Girl" in and around Tombstone. Those who made this claim clearly never consulted a source that would have provided the correct definition of what a silhouette actually is: "a solid shape, usually black, representing the profile of a person or animal mounted against a light contrasting color." Some writers have gone as far to claim that May Leslie gave this as one of the reasons mentioned in her divorce complaint. In fact, there is no mention of anything like that in the divorce document. The earliest version of the "Silhouette Girl" story appeared in the publication of Walter Noble Burns's 1927 highly successful book *Tombstone: An Iliad of the Southwest.* Burns wrote how after their marriage, Buckskin Frank and May "set up housekeeping in a cottage and lived quite happily for a time. But Buckskin Frank found domesticity dull, and sought to vary the drab monotony with piquant novelties." Burns allowed his imagination free rein at this point, writing how he would "surprise his pretty bride by shooting a rose out of her hair or a cup of coffee out of her hand as she brought it in for supper." That much is perhaps possible, but that was not the most daring thing Frank Leslie did. He would stand her against the parlor wall and, "with the neatness of a pencil drawing, outline her figure with bullets fired from across the room. . . ." According to Burns, once the outline of the trusting wife was completed she was "at liberty to step out of her bullet silhouette." Burns then assures his readers that "a portrait of this kind usually required several boxes of cartridges. . . . Then, as a finishing detail, the Michael Angelo [*sic*] of the six-shooter would touch in eyes, nose, and mouth with a few final shots." How many Tombstone citizens were aware of this amazing feat of six-shooter skill? Burns stated that all of Tombstone "in fact, marveled at the artistry of these mural portraits, which remained on the parlor walls for years and were shown with great pride by the citizens to visitors to town, the Leslie serving in lieu of a municipal art gallery. But Mrs. Leslie being of a purely domestic turn, showed her utter lack of artistic appreciation by getting a divorce."[10] One can easily feel the rancor Burns felt in comprehending what a loss those silhouettes were . . . how regretful he felt in not being able to go to that parlor and admire the work of Tombstone's Michelangelo.

Leslie was back in Tombstone on July 11, 1887. The *Epitaph* reported that "Frank Leslie arrived in town last night from his ranch near the Chiricahuas, and reports no Indians in his vicinity, in fact he had not heard of the outbreak until his arrival here."[11] In order to raise the $650 he owed May in her divorce settlement, and to protect what he could of his investment in the Magnolia Ranch, Leslie turned over his share to his partner, Milton E. Joyce. The *Epitaph* noted the transaction with the simple report that "Frank Leslie has disposed of his ranch in the Swishelms to M.E. Joyce."[12]

May Leslie had absolutely no interest in her divorce award of a "one-fourth interest" in the Magnolia Ranch or the thirteen horses and 150 head of cattle that went along with it. Accordingly, she sold her share, as well as the livestock and other items, to Milton E. Joyce for a cash settlement. The transaction was published and said "Deeds—May Leslie to M.E. Joyce, all rights, title and interest Magnolia Ranch, Swisshelm Mountains; and claim or demand to horses, cattle, wagons, furniture, fixtures, $711.50."[13]

Leslie remained at the Magnolia Ranch after selling his share of the property to Joyce. It is not known if he bought his shares back from Joyce, once May Leslie no longer had any claims on the property, or if he simply remained at the ranch as an employee. Either way, it continued to be identified as his property in news reports including an *Epitaph* item that said, "Frank Leslie arrived in town from his ranch last night [July 16, 1887] and reports too much rain. He was kicking because his baggage had not arrived, and that he looked like a very poor cowboy because he carried considerable Sulpher Springs valley real estate on his person. He says that the country for stockmen this year is certainly safe, as they have even more rain than wanted. He says that the Sulphur Springs valley is more or less flooded."[14]

On September 10, 1887, it was reported "Judge Peel has disposed of his interest in the Fashion Saloon to Johnny Dean, who has been conducting that popular resort for some time. Johnny is a thorough saloon man, and good boy as well."[15] Once John Ralph "Johnny" Dean bought the Fashion Saloon, he lost no time hiring Frank Leslie to serve drinks on the night shift. According to the *Tombstone Prospector*, "Frank Leslie, night bartender at the Fashion Saloon is building up a fine trade for that popular resort."[16]

On January 17, 1888, the *Tombstone Prospector* reported that Leslie came down with a serious case of pneumonia. It was serious enough to keep him out of the papers for some time. The following month Johnny Dean sold the Fashion Saloon to Louis Vidal and G.S. Bradshaw. The Fashion Saloon, under the new management, opened on February 4, 1888. The *Tombstone Weekly Epitaph* noted that "the Fashion Saloon will be opened tonight with a barbequed sheep and a fine line of liquors and cigars."[17] It is not known if Leslie stayed on as night bartender, or if he was still suffering from pneumonia.

Most of 1888 was a quiet year for Leslie—at least as far as newspaper reports were concerned. Toward the end of the year, Leslie, along with a partner named E.L. Simpson, located a claim they called the "Cottonwood." On January 28, 1889, notice was filed on the claim, with Leslie claiming two-thirds interest.[18]

By 1889 Milton E. Joyce was rarely in Tombstone and was spending most of his time looking after his other business interests in California. He was still well-remembered in Tombstone, where on January 21, 1889, a local paper reported that "a reporter for the S. F. *Examiner* has been interviewing the sporting men of San Francisco on the subject of Pie. M. E. Joyce, formerly of this city, said: 'I have always liked pie. There are some parts of Arizona where pies are used as currency. I have known instances where they have been stacked up on gaming tables, and they were just as good as gold.'"[19]

Joyce had married a second time to a woman named Louisa Mockler on February 27, 1889. A Los Angeles paper reported a honeymoon visit to that city by saying "Colonel M.E. Joyce, of San Francisco, is a sojourner at the Nadeau House, accompanied by his charming bride. The Colonel says that southern California is the ideal region to spend a honeymoon."[20]

The *Tombstone Prospector* claimed that the Magnolia Ranch was up for sale when it reported that "Johnnie Dean, Frank Leslie and the San Francisco gentleman who has been inspecting the ranch belonging to

Leslie & Joyce with a view of purchasing it, came in last night [April 5, 1889]. The sale has, we understand, been perfected."[21]

Birdie Woods, with whom Leslie had had an affair nearly three years earlier, was back in the news on May 28, 1889. She was in Silver City, New Mexico, when her husband, Dick Woods, attacked her with a knife. According to a New Mexico paper called the *Sierra County Advocate*: "Dick Woods, well known in Central and Lordsburg, spent Sunday [May 26, 1889] night in jail in Silver City. He was arrested for cutting Birdie Woods. It seems that Birdie had a handkerchief wrapped around her left hand. Dick asked where she got it. She answered 'A friend gave it to me.' Dick then said, 'Take it off, or I'll cut it off.' Dick carried out his threat and in doing so severely cut the woman's hand."[22]

Birdie Woods may have no longer been an option, but Leslie didn't lack for female company following his divorce. A woman named Mollie Edwards agreed to move in with him at his ranch as his "wife." [23] The relationship between these two ended on July 10, 1889, when Leslie brought a whole new meaning to his reputation of being a "lady killer." The *Tombstone Daily Epitaph* gave this account of what happened:

> Wm. Reynolds arrived in this city yesterday [July 11] morning about 11 o'clock from Horseshoe valley in the Swisshelm mountains, and reported that a man and a woman had been shot by Frank Leslie last Wednesday [July 10] evening at Leslie's ranch. The following are the facts, as far as can be ascertained:
>
> Frank Leslie, who is well known in Tombstone, and who has a ranch in the Swisshelm mountains, came to this city to celebrate the Fourth, leaving James Neil to take care of his ranch during his absence.
>
> He was accompanied by a woman familiarly known as "Mollie," who has been living at the ranch for several months. While here Leslie drank a great deal and did not leave for his ranch until last Tuesday [July 9] morning. He and the woman arrived at the ranch Wednesday night and after remaining a short time Leslie

mounted a horse and went to the house of Reynolds, about a mile and a half away.

He was heavily armed and told Reynolds that he had come to kill him and then intended to clean out the entire valley, at the same time throwing one of his pistols on the ground and telling Reynolds to pick it up and defend himself. Reynolds made no motion to pick up the weapon and made light of the action and Leslie finally left, firing his revolver at intervals until he was out of hearing. Reynolds thought no more of the matter and went to bed.

Next morning he heard a cry for help and discovered Neil, who was badly wounded and scarcely able to talk. After being taken into the house and made as comfortable as possible, Neil said that the night before when Leslie returned from Reynolds' house he came into the room where Neil and the woman were talking and without a warning said: "I'll settle this!" and fired at the woman who fell from the chair without uttering a sound. Leslie then turned and fired two shots at Neil, the first taking effect in his left breast, near the nipple, and the other hitting him in the arm. He was unarmed and got out of the way [escaped] as soon as possible.

He soon became too weak to walk and it took him the remainder of the night to traverse the mile and a half to where aid could be procured. While dressing Neil's wounds Reynolds observed that the one in the breast had not bled externally, but from the labored breathing and weak tone of voice it was evident that his chest was nearly filled with blood. As soon as possible he [Reynolds] started for this city for medical aid, making the trip of over fifty miles in less than five hours.

Dr. Goodfellow left for the scene shortly afterward and a carriage was also sent to convey the living, if any, to this city. Very little hope is entertained that Neil will be alive when the physician arrives, and as Leslie is known to be a good shot it is supposed that the woman is also dead.

The officers were notified and Deputy Sheriff [Enoch A.] Shattuck sent J. Krigbaum, as a special deputy, to look for Leslie. The general

> opinion is that Leslie will not be found alive, as he has either blown his brains out or escaped either into Mexico or New Mexico. Further particulars will probably not be received until the return of Dr. Goodfellow this evening [July 12].
>
> Neil has been working for Reynolds for some time and was of a sober and industrious disposition. Leslie is known throughout Southern Arizona and Mexico, having been a scout under General Crook. When sober he is gentlemanly and courteous, but when drinking is disagreeable and always ready to use his pistol. He killed a man in this city several years ago but was acquitted.[24]

The badly wounded man was still alive and was brought back to Tombstone by Dr. Goodfellow on July 12, 1889. On the same date Leslie was brought into Tombstone by some lawmen and lodged in jail. *The Arizona Weekly Citizen* gave this report:

> The *Tombstone Epitaph* says that Dr. Goodfellow returned from the scene of the recent shooting at Frank Leslie's ranch yesterday. He found that the woman had been shot in the left breast, the bullet passing through the chest and coming out on the right side, causing nearly instant death. The doctor found James Neil at Reynolds' ranch, severely wounded, the ball having passed through the left breast and lodged under the skin on the back. The left arm was shattered by a bullet and was in bad condition. The doctor dressed the wounds and brought the injured man to the city, where he is being cared for at the Cochise Hotel. He will probably recover. Justice Eaton summoned a coroner's jury yesterday and went to the ranch. He will probably return today [July 13].
>
> Last Evening Ben James and a deputy started out to search for Leslie and met him a few miles out of town in company with J.S. Taylor and a young man named [F.W.] Heyne, whom Leslie had told he was coming to Tombstone to surrender to the authorities. He quietly accompanied the officers to jail and was locked up.
>
> Neil was able to talk last evening and told his story substantially the same as published in yesterday's *Epitaph*. Leslie shot at the

> woman twice and probably three times, two of the shots taking effect as stated above.
>
> Leslie denies any knowledge of the shooting.[25]

Although his name is usually spelled "Neil" in the newspaper accounts, his actual surname was "Neal." At the "Inquest held on the Body of Mollie Edwards" on July 14, 1889, in Tombstone. James B. Neal gave this testimony:

> Q. Please state your name and age.
>
> A. My name is James B. Neal. My age is 31 years.
>
> Q. Do you know the ranch known as the "Leslie Ranch."?
>
> A. Yes, sir.
>
> Q. In what county and territory is this ranch?
>
> A. In Cochise County, Arizona Territory.
>
> Q. Are you acquainted with a man known as Frank Leslie?
>
> A. Yes, sir.
>
> Q. How long have you known him?
>
> A. I have known him by reputation for about three years. I have only known him personally about two months.
>
> Q. Were you at the Leslie Ranch on Wednesday night last?
>
> A. I was.
>
> Q. State how you happened to be there.

A. I went down there, from Mr. Reynolds place, to stay there while Leslie went to Tombstone and take care of things while he was gone.

Q. At whose request did you go down there?

A. At Mr. Leslie's request.

Q. At what time did you go there?

A. I think it was about the 2nd day of this month—July.

Q. At what date did Leslie leave the ranch, and at what time did he return home?

A. He left on the 2nd of July, and he came back on Tuesday the 9th.

Q. Did he have anybody with him when he went away and when he returned?

A. He had a woman with him. The only name I ever heard for her was "Mollie." Leslie claimed her to be his wife.

Q. State if [you] know whether any injuries happened to this woman after she got back there.

A. The first evening they got back all was peace and harmony. There was no trouble until Wednesday evening, that I know of. When the sun was about half on the grass high [?], Leslie says to me "I failed to get any money out of Reynolds this time. He paid me $6 in money." He [Leslie] did have $10 but they spent some of it in town.

He then said to me "Did Reynolds get the rod for the pump?" I told him I did not think he did, for I would have seen it if it had been there on his buckboard. He then asked me if I had ever heard Reynolds say whether he would or would not buy the pump from him. I told him that I had heard Mr. Reynolds say that Mr. Leslie asked $28 for it and Reynolds said he did not think he could give that much for an old pump.

He said that Reynolds had been owing him some money for some time, and now he did not care whether the son of a bitch paid for it or not; that he was going right up there and if there was any fight in him he was going to get it out of him. He said he was going to kill him (Reynolds), that he was going to make a clean up in the valley, that he did not want him there in his way. He went in the house then and got his jacket and put it on and turned around to me and said "I will leave Mollie in your charge till I come back."

He got on his horse and struck out up toward Mr. Reynolds ranch. He was not gone but a few minutes—10 or 15 minutes I reckon, when the woman Mollie came out of the house and fired a shot gun off, and called for me. She heard Frank firing his pistol off and she wanted me to go with her to Reynolds. I told her he was shooting his pistol off this side of Reynolds, that he was not at Reynolds at all. We started and went about 100 yards and met Frank coming back.

He got down off his horse and told me that Reynolds would not make any fight at all. That he wouldn't do nothing. The woman got on the horse and rode him down to the tank at the mill and watered him. She came back to the house and got some chairs and brought them out on the platform on the east side of the house. She sat down and Frank and myself sat on the chairs.

He then gave me a history of his neighbors—Reynolds and Stewart—and how they had treated him. Don't remember all that he did say. We talked about matters in the neighborhood. He said he wanted me to stay with him. He then asked Mollie if she had any whiskey left in the bottle. She told him she had a little left and went and brought it out. He and the woman drunk what there was. I did not drink any of it.

Leslie and the woman commenced quarreling about her not being left in town for a couple of weeks, as he had arranged to do. They then would fight a spell and then he would get on his knees and beg her pardon. This thing was repeated five or six times. She got up and sat down on the tub. She told Frank that she had been one of the girls about town and was done with Frank and that all she wanted was to go back to town.

Leslie jumped up like as if he was going to strike he and says "I won't hit anyone with my fists," and went in the house and got his pistol and came out with it on the platform and fired at Mollie. He then turned right around and shot me. After he fired that first I said "Frank, good God, what is the matter with you?" He said "That was nothing. They were blank cartridges." He then fired two more shots at me. Then he went back into the house. When he did this I lit out for Reynolds ranch.

When I got to the saddle room at the west end of the house I saw through the fence that the woman, Mollie, was lying on her face or side on the ground. I pulled out as fast as I could and went to the Reynolds ranch. This was between nine and ten o'clock at night. I got off [lost] my way and did not get there till next morning. When I got there I told Reynolds that Leslie had shot me and the woman also. Reynolds started in a few minutes for Tombstone.

Q. What weapon did Leslie use in doing the shooting?

A. I think it was an ivory handled pistol. .41 caliber.

Q. Did he shoot both the woman and you with the same pistol?

A. It was the same pistol.

Q. When Leslie first began the shooting of the woman did he have a cartridge belt with him?

A. I don't think he did. He just carried the pistol.

Q. Was the woman sitting on the porch, or platform, of the house when Leslie shot her?

A. She was at the north east corner of the house right close to the corner of the house. She was standing up and threw up her hands and came around when he fired, as Leslie shot at me. I saw the woman leave the corner of the house and go around it out of sight.

Q. Were you sitting at the time?

A. I was near a water barrel at the gate, possibly leaning against the water barrel.

Q. Did you or the woman have any kind of weapon with you at the time of the shooting you have described?

A. I had none as far as I know. She had none. All I had was a pocket knife in my pocket.

Q. State whether Leslie came to Reynolds ranch, after you got there, and what happened that you know of ?

A. He came there an hour after I got in there and asked Mr. [Leroy] Moody if he had "seen anything of Jim," and Moody said no. Leslie then said that I had shot Mollie and he was was going to kill me. Moody came down and told me that Leslie was looking for me and if he saw me he would kill me. I was sitting in the tent with a double barreled shotgun loaded with buck shot and with another gun under the table, pointing at the entrance of the tent.

Leslie talked there a good while. I could not tell all he said. Moody came down to the tent again and told me "Jim, I am afraid if he comes here, he will come in and commence shooting at you." I then got up and left the table and went to the house and set down. Leslie and Moody were then uphill in the other tent above me. Moody then told me he was going with Powers [to get Leslie]. When Moody, Powers and others got back there Leslie had left.[26]

Four days after the killing, on July 14, the coroner's jury returned their verdict that found "after inspecting the body of the deceased and hearing the testimony we find that the person killed was formerly known as Mollie Edwards; that at the time of her death Frank Leslie claimed her as his wife; that on Wednesday, the 10th day of July, 1889, at a place in Cochise County known as 'Leslie's Ranch,' she came to her death by being shot with a pistol and by criminal means; and that she was, on the day aforesaid, shot and killed by Frank Leslie." [27]

The *Tombstone Daily Prospector* published an article headlined "Leslie's Hearing," on July 15, 1889, which raised some interesting questions concerning Buckskin Frank's antecedents:

> Frank Leslie was brought before Judge Easton this morning, but stated that he was not ready to plead, and asked for time to consult a lawyer. It is said that either Mark Smith, Allen English, or both of them, will take the case. He was remanded to jail and will probably have a hearing sometime during the week.
>
> Leslie was born in Galveston, Texas, and although giving his name as Franklin [*sic*] Nashville Leslie his father's name was Kennedy. He has an uncle residing in Houston who is very wealthy, and owns much property there. His name is Thomas Kennedy. Leslie's mother's maiden name was Leslie, and after her death he had trouble with his father and left home taking the name of his mother's family afterward.
>
> Leslie has the appearance this morning of not feeling in the best of spirits. He has probably had time to reflect upon the cowardly crime he has committed in shooting a defenseless woman through the heart.[28]

On July 16 the *Epitaph* reported that "Frank Leslie was taken before Justice Easton yesterday morning for a preliminary examination. He was unable to secure the services of an attorney and waived a hearing and was remanded to the custody of the Sheriff. He will remain in the county jail until the grand jury meets next November."[29]

While Leslie was still in jail awaiting trial, Birdie Woods was back in Tombstone, performing her act and pulling in the crowds. According to the *Epitaph,* "the concert hall was crowded last night [August 31, 1889] to welcome the reappearance of Miss Birdie Woods, who has so far recovered from her illness as to make the concert hall resound with melody."[30]

Thirty-three-year-old May Leslie, the wife Leslie cheated on with Miss Birdie Woods, decided to try marriage for a third time. On October 12, 1889, she married thirty-five-year-old Alexander Durward in Tombstone. The ceremony took place at the bride's residence on Fourth Street, not far from the jail where Leslie was being held. The following day the *Epitaph* reported that "the ceremony was performed last evening by Reverend C. F. Spray . . . with only a few intimate friends being present. We acknowledge a generous supply of wine, wedding cake and other sweetmeats, and, although we are somewhat disfigured [*sic*, disappointed?], we join with the many friends of the happy couple in wishing them a happy future and hope that their lives may never be marred by a single regret."[31] The third time was the charm for May Killeen Leslie Durward. This marriage was a successful one.

The following month, on November 29, 1889, while Leslie was still in the Tombstone jail, Milton E. Joyce died in San Francisco, from tuberculosis, at the age of forty-two. The next day a San Francisco paper printed an obituary stating that "Milton E. Joyce, formerly proprietor of the Baldwin Billiard Parlor and at the time of his decease owner of the Café Royal, died at his residence on Van Ness Avenue at an early hour yesterday morning. He was but forty-two years of age. When fifteen years of age he came to California and settled at Halfmoon Bay, San Mateo county, where he later had a black-smith shop. He went to Arizona, where he accumulated a fortune. In 1883 he formed a partnership with James W. Orndorff and opened the Baldwin Billiard Parlor. They remained there four years when Baldwin made up his mind to take charge of the saloon and billiard room himself. Joyce and Orndorff then established the Café Royal, where they have since remained."[32]

Joyce's death couldn't have happened at a worse time, as far as Leslie was concerned. Four days after Joyce's death the *Tombstone Prospector* reported that "Frank Leslie, who is in the jail here awaiting the action of the grand jury on a charge of murder, was firm in the belief that M.E. Joyce would help him out of his difficulty."[33] Milton E. Joyce was a very wealthy man, in 1889 dollars, when he died. One California paper mentioned that his widow, "Mrs. Louisa M. Joyce has petitioned for letters of administration upon the $30,000 estate of Milton E. Joyce."[34]

On December 27, 1889, the *Tombstone Prospector* reported that "the grand jury made a partial report and presented three indictments, two against Frank Leslie, respectively for murder and assault with intent to commit murder, and one against George Wood for burglary. Leslie was given to the 30th to plead and Wood plead guilty and will be sentenced tomorrow."[35] The following day the same paper reported that "Wm. Staehle was appointed by the court as attorney for Frank Leslie, whose case will come up on Monday next."[36] Leslie was brought into court on December 30 and entered a plea of not guilty. A trial date was then set for January 2, 1890.

Pulp writers and serious writers alike have concluded that alcohol had finally got the best of Leslie when he murdered Mollie Edwards on July 10, 1889. The truth seems to be more complicated than that—at least according to Leslie himself. On January 2, 1890, Leslie's trial for the murder of Mollie Edwards was supposed to begin, but his attorney made a motion for a postponement, which was supported by a signed affidavit from Leslie. This affidavit is an important document that sheds new light on Leslie's mental and physical condition, told in his own words. It is given here in full:

In the District Court of the First Judicial District of the

Territory of Arizona, in and for the County of Cochise

Territory of Arizona v Frank Leslie

Assault with Intent to Murder

Affidavit for Postponement of Trial

Frank Leslie being duly sworn, and deposed says:—That he is the defendant in the above entitled action. That he has fully and fairly stated the case in this action to Wm. Staehle, his counsel, who resides in Tombstone, A.T., and he is advised by his said counsel, and verily believes, that he has a good and substantial defense to said action on the merits. That he cannot safely go to trial at this term of this Court, on account of his inability to show the consequences on his brain, of two gunshot wounds penetrating affiant's skull, in the treatment of which wounds fragments of skull bone were removed, also two other wounds on skull, one of which an arrow wound received in the U.S. Service as Courier under Gen. Custer, which said wounds were all received prior to the commission of the alleged offence in effect producing in affiant the symptoms of [*illegible*] disease, in this, that he is highly sensitive to sounds, frequent flushings and pallor alternately, intense headaches for three years last past, and irresistible muscular movements. Affiant verily believes that he has insane impulses on occasion, due to consequential injuries to his brain arising from said wounds or either of them, and that he deems himself suffering from a form of mania, which he can only show in his defense by a medical expert, to draw the conclusions from careful and frequent examinations of affiant.

That the evidence is material for defendant's defense; and due diligence since the finding of the indictment unable to procure the medical attendance requisite, affiant having no available means.

Affiant further says that he can, after the appointment of an administrator in the matter of the estate of M.E. Joyce deceased, (for which letters have been applied in the Probate Court of Cochise County and set for hearing January 13th 1890 at 10 a.m.) present his claim against said estate, and be enabled to engage such professional attendance and examination of said disease, with full liberty on the part of the Court to appoint a regular, duly licensed, practicing physician as [*two words illegible*] at the pleasure of the Court. That he expects to prove by said testimony thus obtained that he was at the time of the commission of said offense capable of committing the offense charged without being conscious thereof.

That said facts cannot to his knowledge be shown and safely established in any other manner.

This application is made in good faith and not for delay merely, but that justice may be done as the [*illegible*] affiant verily believes that if this cause be continued from this Term of the Court, he will be able to present his defense as above stated at the next Term of Court.

N. F. LESLIE

Sworn to before me this 2nd day of Jan. 1890.

GEO. H. DAILY

Clerk, Dist. Court [37]

The following day, the *Tombstone Prospector* gave a report stating that "the case of the Territory vs. Leslie was called for 2 o'clock and at that time the court room was crowded with a curious throng. They were disappointed however, for the case was continued to Monday [January 6], on a motion of Wm. Staehle, the defendant's attorney who outlined the defense by asking for a continuance until a prominent Los Angeles physician could arrive whose testimony would show the defendant to have spells of insanity under certain conditions and his irresponsibility at the time of the killing."[38]

There is no record of the "prominent Los Angeles physician" actually appearing in court on Leslie's behalf. Most likely he wouldn't have been able to get to Tombstone in time, since Attorney William C. Staehle's motion to continue Leslie's trial at a later date was overruled by the Judge. On January 6, 1890, Leslie withdrew his plea of not guilty and pleaded guilty to murder. The sudden conclusion of his trial was reported in several newspapers. A California journal reported simply that Frank Leslie, better known as "Buckskin Frank" who had shot and killed a woman who was living on his ranch, had entered the court and entered plea of guilty to murder in the first degree. A life sentence at Yuma was anticipated to be the punishment. Remarkably, the newspaper pointed out that "Leslie was noted for his bravery during the Custer massacre, when he was in the employment of the Government as a scout, and rendered valuable services to the Government under Crook and Miles in this section during the campaign of Geronimo and his band of cut-throats." How many readers believed Leslie had had any involvement with General Custer is anybody's guess. It was accepted that he had been a scout during the Apache wars. One other fact worthy of mention is that Leslie "was a partner to the late M.E. Joyce, of the Baldwin Hotel, in a large cattle ranch in this country."[39]

Chapter 11

Convict No. 632 at Yuma

As predicted, Leslie was sentenced to a life term in prison. On January 10, 1890, he was escorted to the prison at Yuma and logged in as convict No. 632. In reporting Leslie's arrival, the *Arizona Sentinel* noted that "the eleven convicts who were brought here from Tombstone yesterday arrived in an intoxicated condition. One of the number, a life prisoner, Frank Leslie, was so drunk that he could hardly walk." [1] Leslie had been brought to the Yuma penitentiary by Sheriff John Horton Slaughter of Cochise County and Deputy Sheriff Hugh Taylor.

It didn't take long for Slaughter and his deputy to respond to the assertion by the *Arizona Sentinel* that the convicts had been delivered in "an intoxicated condition." According to the *Tombstone Prospector,* the "Yuma *Sentinel* published an item last Saturday to the effect that the eleven prisoners taken down there were all drunk when they arrived. From the deputies who took them there it is learned that the assertion is positively false in every particular. The men were all in a perfectly sober condition, and the report that Frank Leslie was drunk to an extent that he could not walk probably arose from the fact that he was very weak when he left here and was assisted by two deputies when he arrived at Yuma from the depot to the prison."[2] The *Epitaph* chimed in with the

Prospector by noting that "the idea that a sheriff and one deputy would allow a gang of eleven men to get drunk on their way to prison, outside of being extremely absurd would be very dangerous."[3]

After delivering Leslie to the prison, Sheriff Slaughter and Deputy Sheriff Taylor continued on to Los Angeles. Their arrival there, on January 13, was reported by the *Los Angeles Times*, which noted that "Sheriff J.H. Slaughter of Cochise County, Ariz., and his deputy, Hugh Taylor, were in the city yesterday. They brought up and left at the Yuma Penitentiary N.F. Leslie, *a man formerly known in Los Angeles*, [authors' italics] to serve out a life sentence for murder."[4]

The official prison record for Leslie, at the time he entered Yuma, stated that "his height is given as 5 feet 7 ¼ inches, 135 in weight. He wore a size 5 boot. At the time of incarceration, he was single. He was blue-eyed, dark-haired, fair-skinned, intemperate, could read and write, and smoked tobacco. He was a native of the state of Texas and was 48 years of age when received." [5]

There was another prisoner from Tombstone who, within days, followed Leslie into Yuma. Of all people, the new convict turned out to be Dick Woods—the husband of Birdie Woods. The *Santa Fe New Mexican* printed a dispatch from Silver City that said "Dick Woods, well known in Grant County, who cut Birdie Woods in the hand in this city [Silver City, New Mexico] last summer, is now in jail in Tombstone. He plead guilty to grand larceny, for which he received three years in the Yuma penitentiary."[6]

Leslie was in the Yuma prison less than three months when he joined five other convicts in an escape attempt. According to the *Arizona Daily Citizen*, "Frank Leslie, together with five other of his companions, came very near escaping from the penitentiary the other day. Frank Leslie was the poor individual who was sentenced to the state prison for life, for nothing more than wantonly murdering a defenseless woman. He had almost dug his way out but one of the convicts who was party to the scheme weakened and notified a guard."[7]

Leslie was sent to solitary for his part in the escape attempt. Once he was allowed to return to the general prison population, he became a model prisoner, who found employment as a pharmacist in the prison infirmary. The best account of what life was like for Leslie as a Yuma prisoner was published in one of Tombstone's newspapers on July 25, 1890. Parts of it read as if it were written by a member of the Chamber of Commerce. "Yuma has one institution beside the admirably conducted hotel and two papers—the *Times* and the *Sentinel*—which she may very well feel proud of." After these words of praise the writer resorts more to honest journalism. "The penitentiary is an institution of which few people, aside from those who have to go there, have any idea, outside of the knowledge that it is a prison. The convicts there number 143 at the present time. The prison grounds and buildings proper are surrounded by an adobe wall of formidable dimensions. The description of the walls, guard houses, Gatling gun stand and other perfectly arranged means of thwarting any attempt at escape are a secondary consideration to the comfort and well being of the prisoners confined within the walls." Mention of a Gatling gun and other items to thwart "any attempt at escape" certainly reminded the reader what the purpose of Yuma prison was. But additional information reassured the reader it was not a hell-hole. "In the first place the visitor is struck with the remarkably cool atmosphere throughout the interior of the building. The ventilation is perfect. The bath room where any one of the convicts can take a shower bath at any time of day, the library with its extensive shelves piled with books, the barber shop, drug department, laundry and other conveniences, for the health and comfort of the prisoners, are models in their manner of construction and accessories." Surprisingly, for those who have the typical stereotype of what a prison is like, Yuma proved the exception as the reporter continued. "The prisoners are not confined in their cells all day as is the case with many prisons, but are allowed to mingle with each other with perfect freedom. The library is well patronized and is filled with a class of books instructive as well as interesting. The prisoners are allowed to choose any occupation they may desire. Some of them busy themselves in making canes, bureaus, and wood ornaments, others with lace work. There is an air of happiness and a contented feeling among the men which is a pleasing surprise. The surroundings are of a much cleaner and more civilized type than a large number of the men were used to when they had their freedom. Among those known in Tombstone who are confined here Sam McClaren who has charge of the kitchen; his brother who assists him; Wilson Douglass who aids assistant Hatch on his rounds, night and morning and Frank Leslie, who dispenses medicine to the patients."[8]

During September 1890 the *Tombstone Prospector* reported that "several letters have been sent to Tombstone by the mother of the young woman who was killed by Frank Leslie, asking whether the latter or either of them had any property."[9] No further reports have been found that would identify who "the mother" was, and where she came from.

On December 6, 1890, the *Tombstone Prospector* reported that "the Joyce estate was sold yesterday to Si Bryant for the sum of $4500. Si made up his mind to buy it a few weeks ago and took a couple of carloads of ore to Socorro and returned yesterday with over $6000 in his pocket, $4500 of which he planked down to E.A. Shattuck, the administrator of the estate. The ranch is the well-known Leslie Ranch, known as Silver Creek, between the Swisshelm and Chiricahua mountains. The purchase embraces all of the horses and cattle on the range." That same issue of the *Tombstone Prospector* also contained a "Certificate of Sale" which said that the "Seven-Up" brand owned by "N.F. Leslie" was being sold to "E.A. Shattuck, administrator" for $10.[10]

Louisa M. Joyce, the widow of Leslie's friend Milton E. Joyce, was having money issues of her own during November 1891. According to the *San Francisco Chronicle*, "Judge Levy has denied a motion made by a sister of the late Milton E. Joyce to reduce the allowance to the widow, Louisa Joyce, from $150 to $100 a month."[11] Besides her sister-in-law, the widow Joyce was also having a financial dispute with James Wilson Orndorff, her husband's former business partner and the man who would later provide a bed and board for Leslie during his final years. During December 1891 the *Chronicle* reported that "Judge Garber has denied the motion to place the Café Royal in the hands of a receiver pending the trial of the suit of Louisa M. Joyce, admistratrix [*sic*] of the estate of Milton E. Joyce, to recover $7200 claimed to be due from James Orndorff, the surviving partner."[12]

Louisa Joyce's suit against James Wilson Orndorff dragged into 1892, when Orndorff responded to her suit. According to the *San Francisco Chronicle* "James W. Orndorff of the Café Royal has filed an answer to the suit brought by the widow of the deceased partner, Milton E. Joyce, for an alleged balance on an account. Orndorff denies that he owes the Joyce estate $7221 or any other sum, or that his management of the business is now or will continue to work injury and loss to the plaintiff."[13]

Occasionally, Louisa Joyce's name appeared as "Louise" in reports of her suit, such as this example from May 17, 1892, which said that "Judge Garber granted a trial jury in the case of Louise M. Joyce, administrator of the estate of Milton E. Joyce, against James W. Orndorff, surviving partner in the Café Royal, and denied the accounting, but with the privilege of renewing the motion if the partnership business is not wound up in thirty days."[14]

James Wilson Orndorff got tired of the legal proceedings. On May 26, 1892, the *San Francisco Call* reported that "James Orndorff, surviving partner of Milton E. Joyce, has decided to sell the Café Royal billiard parlors by auction, being unable to effect a private sale. The sale will be made by order of Judge Garber to wind up the partnership business of the firm of Joyce & Orndorff."[15] This still did not end the legal battles between Orndorff and Louisa Joyce, which would take nearly two more years to resolve.

W.H. Cameron, a reporter for the *San Francisco Chronicle*, interviewed Leslie at the Yuma Penitentiary during December 1893 and concluded that "his lot in prison is not a hard one. He does not wear the prison garb and is not confined to a cell at night. His conduct is perfect. Superintendent

[Thomas] Gates said that he was the best-behaved prisoner, as well as the most useful in the penitentiary. In case of sickness the physician is called in and diagnoses the case, while Leslie fills the prescription and administers the medicine. His drug store is the acme of neatness."[16]

After reading Cameron's *San Francisco Chronicle* article, a thirty-six-year-old divorcée named Belle Stowell, then living in San Francisco, began corresponding with Leslie. The letters continued after her return to her home in Warren County, Illinois, which was the same county in Illinois where Wyatt Earp had been born. From her home in Illinois, Belle Stowell began planning a campaign to have Leslie pardoned.

During March 1894, the long legal battle fought in the San Francisco courts between James W. Orndorff and Louisa Joyce finally came to an end. "Victory For Orndorff" was the headline used by the *San Francisco Chronicle* when they reported that "Judge Sanderson has decided that James Orndorff of the Café Royal is not bound by the declaration of his partner, Milton E. Joyce, in the latter's will that Orndorff owed the partnership some $7000. The petition of Joyce's widow to have this amount declared as representing an account stated up to the time of her husband's death was denied. . . . An expert who has examined the books finds that Orndorff owed the firm little or nothing. The books were kept by Joyce."[17]

A journalist named J.M. Burnett visited the Yuma penitentiary during April 1894, and wrote an article for the *Arizona Sentinel* that provided another look at Leslie's life as Convict No. 632:

> Entering one room, a convict arose from a couch, quietly unlocked four doors which formed a part of a partition, and, throwing these doors open disclosed a complete, neat and full stocked drugstore. Not a speck of dirt or particle of dust on shelf or bottle, yet this gazelle-eyed, girl featured, mild voiced young man, in manner and language denoting refinement and education, begged us to excuse the untidy appearance of things because he had been for a few days suffering from an attack of la grippe. He won our heart

> in two seconds, and had we the pardoning power, well—we don't know what we would have done. Upon inquiry we learned that he was Frank Leslie, at one time a chief of scouts, had cold-blooded murders marked up for his record, and who, if liberated, would in all probability add to the list in a very short time.[18]

J.M. Burnett's description of Leslie as "this gazelle-eyed, girl featured, mild voiced young man" is certainly at odds with the image usually associated with rough-hewn plainsmen and gunfighters. It is interesting that Burnett, who appeared close to being smitten with his subject, described Leslie as "mild voiced young man." Leslie was often taken for someone much younger than his actual age. At the time Burnett visited his prison drugstore, Leslie had just turned fifty-two.

The man who was almost killed when Leslie murdered Mollie Edwards was back in the news nearly five years later. During June 1894, the *Tombstone Weekly Epitaph* provided an update that said "James Neal came in last night [June 16, 1894] from the Golden Rule mine where he has been doing assessment work on the Mountain Key claim. He was the last man to leave the camp. He will take his departure in a day or two for Indian Territory. Mr. Neal, it will be remembered, is the man who was left for dead by Frank Leslie . . . who shot Neal and then killed his (Leslie's) mistress, for which crime he is serving a life term in the penitentiary."[19]

On January 19, 1895, the *Arizona Weekly Citizen* published a lengthy article entitled "Territorial Penitentiary a Comfortable and Well Managed Institution," which contained profiles of several prisoners including this one of Leslie:

> Some of the prisoners there have strong personalities. There is Frank Leslie of Tombstone, who years ago killed a woman he was living with, and shot his ranch foreman, a man named Neal. He is a model prisoner. He has charge of the drug department, handles it to perfection, making no mistakes, intentionally or otherwise. He is of fine education, and a smart man—smart enough to be a first class prisoner.

> Years ago in Tombstone he went on a spree and started for his ranch in an ugly mood. He shot and killed the woman who lived with him in some dispute, and then turned and fired on Neal, who witnessed the deed. Neal was not killed, though he was badly hurt. He managed to crawl outside, and so sure was Leslie that he had killed him that he did [not] take the trouble to make sure of him. Neal got away and went to Tombstone, where he told of the fray.
>
> Meanwhile Leslie had started for Tombstone, too. On the road he met a deputy sheriff, who was going after him. To him he told that his wife had been shot by Neal, and that Neal had turned his gun on him (Leslie) and but for quick shooting, killing Neal, he, too, would have been killed.
>
> "That's all right, Leslie," said the deputy, "get in here and I'll give you a ride. You are under arrest. Neal is alive, and in town, all right." Leslie collapsed. He begged the deputy to hold off taking him till dark, as they would lynch him. The deputy took him in safely. He was sentenced to life imprisonment, having plead guilty.
>
> His plan now is to be on his best behavior, and keep quiet till the whole affair has been forgotten. Then, on some long future day he will make an effort, and a very strong one, for a pardon.[20]

By 1895 Mrs. Belle Stowell, of Warren County, Illinois, had convinced several people to join with her in her campaign to have Frank Leslie pardoned. Leslie was clearly encouraged by her efforts. On December 8, 1895, the *Tombstone Weekly Epitaph* noted that "Frank Leslie, who was sentenced from Tombstone for life in Yuma for the murder of a woman at his ranch in the Swisshelm mountains, longs for liberty and is now making petition for a pardon. He has served eight [*sic*] years and has been a good working trusty during that time."[21]

During June 1896 the *Tombstone Prospector* reported that "it is probable that Frank Leslie, who was sentenced from this county to Yuma for murder, is likely to soon be a free man, as the Gazette states that executive clemency is to be extended in his behalf by Gov. Franklin."[22] On November

17, 1896, Governor Benjamin J. Franklin of the Territory of Arizona granted Leslie a full and unconditional pardon.

"The application for pardon," Governor Franklin explained, "was recommended very strongly by the present and late prison officials on the ground of his exemplary conduct and the valuable services he has rendered that institution as hospital steward and prison druggist. Dr. Cotter, late prison physician, states that during epidemics when his assistance to the sick deprived him of rest night and day for weeks at a time he never murmured, but was a most humane and self-sacrificing attendant.

"Mr. Leslie's application for pardon is further recommended by many prominent citizens, territorial officials, and U.S. Army Officers, including the Hon. M.A. Smith, and Judge J. J. Hawkins. Lieut. Col. Lawler, of the U.S. Army writes that 'when Arizona was terrorized by the atrocities of the hostile Indian tribes under Geronimo, Mr. Leslie was the first to respond to a call for assistance and gave splendid service to the Army as a scout and guide.'

"He is shown to be a man of good character and education, his only fault being that he occasionally drinks to excess, and was crazed by drink when he committed this crime. I am assured that he has entirely abstained from the use of intoxicating liquors, and although submitted to the strongest temptations as prison druggist, has never betrayed a trust. He plead guilty, but if properly defended I am of the opinion that he would have received a very light sentence. I believe that the ends of justice have been fully served, and that this case merits executive clemency.

"Now, therefore I, Benjamin J. Franklin, by virtue of the power and authority in me vested do hereby grant unto the said Frank Leslie a full and unconditional Pardon and do order that he be set at liberty forthwith."[23]

Dr. George Goodfellow was a longtime Leslie friend, and worked hard to get him pardoned. The day after he pardoned Leslie, Gov. Benjamin J. Franklin wrote Dr. Goodfellow that Buckskin Frank's release "will restore to society an industrious and respected citizen."[24] After he walked out of prison, Leslie caught a train to Stockton, California, where Mrs. Belle Stowell was waiting for him.

Chapter 12

Marriage to Belle Stowell

Leslie and Belle Stowell went to the County Clerk's office in Stockton on December 1, 1896, and signed their names, along with personal information on a marriage license. Leslie identified himself as "Nashville Franklyn Leslie, native of Virginia, age 55," and stated that he was a "resident of San Carlos, Territory of Arizona." His bride described herself as "Mrs. Belle Stowell, native of Warren Co., Illinois, age 39, resident of Warren Co. Illinois."[1]

The following day, the *Stockton Daily Independent* printed a lengthy account of the nuptials headlined "A Chivalrous Scout Weds a Pretty Widow," in which it observed:

> Cupid Fyfe [Deputy County Clerk R.G.W. Fyfe], in his winning way, soon learned considerable of Mr. Leslie's story. He was a widower and the lady who was to meet him was a widow. This was the agreed meeting point, she coming from her home in Illinois and he from Arizona. Their wedding trip was to be to China, the start to be made by the next Steamer . . .
>
> Justice Parker was on hand promptly, and . . . the groom and the bride entered the chambers at the tick of the clock when the hand

> pointed to the hour of 7. Justice Parker put his best touches on the simple civil service provided for the occasion, and the groom with a medieval chivalry gave his bride a kiss of wedlock on the forehead. The bride, who is a pretty little woman, seemed to harbor a profound regard for her husband.
>
> Before he left the groom did not fail to remember the Justice. . . . He took the Justice's address and asked him, not to name the poison, but some article in China, say an Oriental walking stick, which would be forwarded to him by the first steamer from the Orient. . . . The couple announced that they would go to San Francisco by last evening's train and would sail for Chang's land on the first steamer.[2]

Not surprisingly, the newlyweds never caught that first steamer to China. Their next press notice was reported by the *San Francisco Call* who reported the appearance of a detective who turned up in Stockton on April 21, 1897:

> Stockton, Cal., April 21. —On December 1 last Nashville Franklyn Leslie, giving his residence as San Carlos, Ariz. took out a license in this city to marry Mrs. Belle Stowell, whose residence was put down upon the license as Warren County, Ill. He and the woman thereupon sought out Justice Parker and were wedded. Leslie told the Justice a romantic story, but it was not half as romantic as the truth would have been. He said he was an Indian scout, and stated further that he and his bride were going to China for a honeymoon trip. He promised to send the Justice a curiously wrought cane from the Orient as a memento.
>
> Nothing more was heard of the couple until this forenoon, when a San Francisco detective walked into the County Clerk's office and asked to see the stub of the license book. He then called upon Justice Parker and the true romance became known.
>
> Leslie was an Indian scout, as he represented himself to be, but he came to Stockton direct from the Territorial prison in Yuma county, Arizona. He exchanged the stripes for a wedding dress. He had just just served eight years for murder. The detective who

> was looking up Mr. Leslie's record did not remember whether he murdered his wife or a man whom he found with her, but he was under the impression that it was his wife whom he killed.
>
> At that time the San Francisco papers published accounts of Leslie's exploits, and in the biography of the murderer reproduced pictures of him. Mrs. Belle Stowell, who then lived in San Francisco, and who was the ex-wife of a prominent man in the employ of the Southern Pacific Railroad Company, read the narrative of the scout's adventures, and though she had never seen him she became infatuated. She had just been divorced from her husband, and she began to correspond with the murderer. Flowers followed the letters, and then fruit was sent. The murderer reciprocated, or pretended to, and the only hindrance to the marriage was his incarceration.
>
> Mrs. Stowell obtained a railroad pass to Yuma, Ariz., from her ex-husband. He little thought that she was going to join a murderer upon the latter's release from prison, but such was her mission. When Leslie had served out his time he and his bride-to-be came direct to this city, where the license was obtained and the marriage took place.
>
> Mrs. Stowell has been and is still drawing $40 monthly alimony from her former husband. The latter tired of paying her this sum, and the detective's mission here was to obtain evidence whereby the order of alimony might be revoked.
>
> Mrs. Leslie is at present in this State, but it is said that her husband cannot be located, although it is believed that he might be in Randsburg. It is not known whether they have separated or not, but it is believed that they have.[3]

Leslie and Belle had indeed separated. Randsburg, California, was a mining camp that had just had a major gold strike. While Leslie might have considered going to Randsburg, he went to Fort Worth, Texas, instead.

Chapter 13

Fort Worth, Cuba, and Mexico

In Fort Worth Leslie looked up his old friend John Ralph "Johnny" Dean who had employed him at the Fashion Saloon in Tombstone. By now, Dean had outgrown the name "Johnny," and had upgraded himself to "Captain Jack" Dean. A Fort Worth paper reported their April 7, 1897, reunion by saying "Capt. Frank Leslie arrived last evening and is visiting his friend Capt. Jack Dean. These two men ranched together in Arizona [and] other points in the southwest years ago in those days when friends counted for something, and they have formed a friendship that has lasted ever since. Capt. Leslie will probably make Fort Worth his future home."[1]

At this time "Capt. Jack" Dean was the night manager of the Delaware Café, located within Fort Worth's Delaware Hotel. Leslie apparently went to work for Dean again, and was still there on July 13, 1897, when it was reported that "as Captain Frank Leslie was coming down in the Delaware elevator yesterday he met an old friend, Mr. Libb Wallace, a famous frontiersman and cowboy. The two men had not met for a dozen years."[2]

News of Leslie's Fort Worth residence traveled back to Tombstone. Late in September 1897 the *Tombstone Prospector* reported that "Frank Leslie, who was sentenced for life from this county and pardoned by Gov. Franklin, is now at Fort Worth, Texas, connected with a large saloon. A visitor to Tombstone informs the *Prospector* that he met Leslie there, and says although now about 60 years of age he looks hale and hearty. Johnny Dean, also a former well-known Tombstonite, is in the same city and interested with Leslie." [3]

Leslie was still living in Fort Worth on January 17, 1898, when he and a group of men made plans for an Alaskan adventure. The press named this group the Fort Worth Klondikers, which seemed appropriate at the time. It appeared the venture would become a reality with their careful planning. The *Dallas Morning News* reported that the charter of the Copper River Gold Mining and Prospect Company of Fort Worth was finalized and had been sent to Austin in charge of "Capt. N.F. Leslie," F.A. Mason, and Silas L. King. Their purpose was to prospect in the Alaskan gold fields. At a previous meeting the board of directors had elected the following officers: F.A. Mason, president; Capt. N.F. Leslie, vice president; James C. Walton, secretary; Silas L. King, treasurer, and W.T. Camp, home secretary. The sum of $1100 had been deposited in the State National Bank in Fort Worth. The group planning to leave on February 15 was made up of F.A. Mason, Capt. N.F. Leslie, James C. Walton, Silas L. King, and R.D. Maxwell of Fort Worth in addition to Charles Mills of Waltham, Massachusetts, A. C. Triesim of Trenton, New Jersey, J. and Alva Keith "of this state." As for supplies the group would purchase what was needed in Seattle and "the other portion at Edmonton, in British territory."[4]

It would appear that Leslie never actually got to Alaska. During early April 1898, he was in Mexico with a famous friend from his Tombstone days. The report stated that "Doctor George Goodfellow, Tom Selby of San Francisco, and Frank Leslie, are at Hermosillo preparing for a trip to the interior."[5]

Leslie couldn't have stayed long in Mexico, if his claim is truthful that he fought and was wounded in Cuba during the Spanish-American War. According to Leslie, "When [Theodore] Roosevelt commanded his regiment, I enlisted in one of the first companies formed in Arizona and after arriving in Cuba was transferred by my own request to [Major General Henry W.] Lawton's command and remained until the end of Spain's dominion in the Western hemisphere. At the end of the war I returned to Arizona."[6]

Following his alleged war service, Leslie once again appeared in Tombstone early in August 1898, serving in his familiar role as guide. A reporter from the *Tombstone Prospector* found him and his article provides us with of another significant event, one which causes us to doubt portions of what he shared. Portions of his interview are truthful, that the "party of engineers under Prof. E.T. Dumble engaged in making a geological survey of Sonora and this section of Arizona for the S.P. Railroad Company arrived in town today." That Frank Leslie was among the party under Professor Dumble is not in question, nor that he was acting as guide. Nor that Leslie was nearly sixty years of age, and "carries his age well and is claimed by acquaintances that he looks as natural as ever." The question arises with the concluding statements that since "leaving Arizona *Leslie has been in Cuba and returned wounded.* After recovery he joined this surveying party and it is expected they will be engaged hereabouts for several months."[7] [italics by authors]

By November 30, 1898, Leslie was in Nogales, Arizona, serving as the "right hand man" to Professor Edwin Theodore Dumble. The *Border Vidette* reported that he had been there obtaining supplies for an excursion. "A carload of fine large mules and horses passed south yesterday morning en route to Guaymas. They are to be used by Professor E.T. Dumble's geological survey party which is being outfitted at Guaymas for the purpose of making a survey of La Barranca coal fields, in which the Southern Pacific company is interested." Professor Dumble "and his right hand man, Capt. Frank Leslie" have been in Nogales several days making arrangements for a month's stay in the field.[8]

Leslie was still in the vicinity of Guaymas, Sonora, during the late summer of 1899 when he had a close call that was described by *The Oasis*, a Nogales newspaper. The report stated that "word from Ortiz conveys the intelligence that two or three days ago, about three miles west of that station, Captain Frank Leslie, well known all over Arizona, was held up by Yaquis and robbed. They took all his arms, mount etc., and turned him loose afoot." [9]

Back in Nogales, on December 16, 1899, the local paper reported "this morning Captain Frank Leslie was a passenger on the train from the south, en route to California for the Christmas holidays." [10] Three days after this item appeared, Leslie's friend Major General Henry Ware Lawton was killed in the Philippines. When word of Lawton's death reached California, Leslie contacted the editor of the *San Francisco Call* and offered to write a feature on Lawton. The paper not only took him up on his offer, but gave his article an entire page in their Sunday, January 7, 1900, issue. The illustrated article was headlined "Personal Experiences With the Late General Lawton Told by Capt. N. Frank Leslie, His Chief of Scouts in the Apache Campaign." The entire text of the *San Francisco Call* article can be found in "Appendix C." [11]

Leslie had left San Francisco before his article in the *San Francisco Call* was published. On January 1, 1900, he was back in Nogales, Arizona, which bordered Nogales, Sonora, Mexico. The neighboring towns, separated by the international border, were known as the "Line Cities." *The Oasis* of Nogales reported that "Monday evening Captain Frank Leslie came in from California, returning to Sonora from a Christmas vacation in the golden state. He remained at the line cities a day or two." [12]

Following his "Christmas vacation in the golden state," Leslie found employment at Mulatos Mining Company in Mexico. He would not return to the United States until January 1901. His time in Mexico explains why he wasn't recorded on the 1900 United States Federal Census. It also explains why he was *not* the "Frank Leslie" who was one of the "four notorious sharpers" arrested by San Francisco police on November 1, 1900. According to the *San Francisco Call* "four sharp bunko men—Harry Walters, Frank Leslie, T. Estraus and T.E. Galt—were taken into custody yesterday afternoon by officers John Sullivan [and] J.B. Hurd and charged with vagrancy at the city prison. On Thursday they attempted to fleece J.P. Reynolds, a Nevada mining man, but the would be victim from the Sagebrush State was too wily for their graft."[13]

While this other "Frank Leslie" was being arrested in San Francisco, Buckskin Frank was still gainfully employed at the Mulatos Mining Company in Mexico. A Nogales, Arizona, reporter from *The Oasis* went to Mexico to interview Leslie, but just missed him. One January 19, 1901, *The Oasis* published the reporter's story, which said that "Captain Frank Leslie, the noted scout and plainsman, is in the employ of the Mulatos Co. When I reached the camp he had gone out only a few hours before with some investors visiting the property to pilot them to Guerreo, Chihuahua, four days journey distant, where they got rail transportation to Pennsylvania."[14]

Leslie was still working for the Mulatos Mining Company as late as March 14, 1902, when he provided the same Nogales newspaper with an update of the company's activities. The paper reported that "from Captain Frank Leslie, who was up from Mulatos yesterday, *The Oasis* learns that work is progressing upon a big, new cyanide plant, which will have a daily capacity of one thousand ton of ore."[15]

Late in 1902, after more than three years employed by the Mulatos Mining Company in Mexico, Leslie decided to return to San Francisco. He was back in the news because of an article datelined "Phoenix, Ariz. —October 4, 1902," which detailed the lives of several noted Tombstone characters, including Leslie. The lengthy article was picked up by papers across the country. We can only wonder what the then sixty-year-old Leslie thought about the section concerning him, if he actually saw the article. The mistakes in the Leslie portion, italicized by the authors of this book, are an annotator's delight:

> There were many joyous cutthroats around Tombstone in those days. One of the most picturesque was Frank Leslie, otherwise "Buckskin Frank." Leslie was well-to-do, with several thousand head of cattle in the Sulphur Springs Valley. He was a blue-eyed, *dainty*, little fellow. His usual costume was of fringed buckskin, with flaring hat, high boots and spotless linen.
>
> *He rarely drank and never to excess.* He "herded by himself" and affiliated with none of the gangs. All that was known of him was that he had been one of Crook's scouts; that he was a man of marvelous endurance, was a man that *killed Apaches by the score.* During his residence about Tombstone *he added, one by one, seven more to the list of the victims.*
>
> One was a jealous husband, who had called him to account at Bilicke's Hotel. *His last killing was that of a man and two women, at his ranch.* He rode to Tombstone, sixty miles away, and voluntarily placed himself under arrest, averring the deed had been done in self-defense. Though he was the only witness, *he was sentenced to ten years in Yuma, "on general principals* [*sic*]*."*
>
> It was found he had an excellent medical education, so he was made prison druggist. He did not serve out his time. He was pardoned, mainly through the efforts of a wealthy woman of middle age, a friend of years before. *Almost at the prison gate they were married.* The last heard of them *they were living happily on the bride's property in Northern California.*[16]

Chapter 14

San Francisco and the Bay Area

Leslie was back in San Francisco on November 25, 1902, when he accidentally shot himself. The first account of the incident was published under the headline "His Gun Was an Automatic" by the *San Francisco Chronicle.* The *Chronicle* reminded its readers that even though Leslie had spent many years on the frontier as a Government scout he had fallen victim to his own pistol on the twenty-fourth. He had been, up "to a recent date" engaged in mining in Mexico. Not surprisingly he was in the habit of carrying an automatic pistol in his inner vest pocket. The accident happened in a saloon at Market and Ellis Streets. When Leslie stooped over the pistol fell out of his pocket and discharged when it hit the floor. The bullet struck him about four inches above the knee, then passed through the fleshy part of his leg, continued by tearing "his right ear," and then cutting a gash in his scalp. At the Receiving Hospital he was treated by a Dr.Weyer.

"I suppose," said Leslie, "that my friends will tell me I'm not fit to carry a pistol. After forty years on the frontier to be hurt by my own gun, looks like it." The *Chronicle* pointed out that Leslie was sixty-one years of age.[1]

Leslie wouldn't actually turn "61 years of age" until March 18, 1903. The story of Leslie shooting himself was picked up by newspapers from other states. One of the more interesting examples was printed, somewhat belatedly, by the *Idaho Falls Times*, which offered a similar, but more detailed and sometimes conflicting, account:

> THE OLD FRONTIERSMAN'S GUN.
>
> It Went Off and Now Captain Leslie
> Is Minus an Ear.
>
> Captain Frank Leslie, an old frontiersman living at San Francisco, was seriously wounded by the accidental discharge of a pistol a few days ago. While he was in a store he stooped to pick up a piece of paper and as he did so his *revolver* fell to the floor. The weapon had a range of 2,000 yards. It was discharged by the force of the fall, and the bullet struck Leslie in the right leg just above the knee.
>
> The piece of lead penetrated upward about four inches, and then, reappeared, continued its upward flight, *completely severing the right ear* and cutting a severe gash along the side of his head.
>
> Leslie is much chagrined over the nature of the accident. "To think," he said, "that after forty years' fighting with the Indians, and constant exposure to all the dangers of frontier life, I should be nearly killed by my own gun—it's enough to make a man hunt cover. I shall never hear the last of this from my friends.[2]

This accidental shooting of November 25, 1902, added another serious head wound to other significant ones Leslie had received decades earlier. In his January 2, 1890, court affidavit, Leslie claimed the earlier head wounds had resulted in him having "insane impulses on occasion," due to "injuries to his brain arising from said wounds." This latest serious wound from 1902 resulted in "completely severing his right ear and cutting a severe gash along the side of the head." It left him disfigured for life, and certainly would have further threatened his already impaired mental condition.

Although they had been separated since 1897, it had taken almost six years for the marriage of Leslie and his wife Belle to officially end. Leslie had been out of the country, in Mexico, for much of that time and it probably took a while for Belle to track him down. On March 19, 1903 (the day after Leslie's sixty-first birthday) the *San Francisco Call* reported that a divorce was granted to "Belle Leslie from N.F. Leslie for failure to provide."

The San Francisco city directories for 1904 and 1905 listed "Leslie, Nashville F." as living at 122 Seventh Street. He was recorded as being employed as the manager of a grocery store at 7 Dikeman Place, owned by a "Mrs. J. Powell."

Leslie's friend James Wilson Orndorff married his second wife in San Francisco on April 5, 1906. The *San Francisco Chronicle* reported that "James W. Orndorff, formerly proprietor of the Café Royal at Fourth and Market streets, was married yesterday to Miss Gussie Hall of 1008 Market Street. The ceremony was performed by Justice Van Nostrand at his chambers in the City Hall. In applying for the marriage license Orndorff gave his age as 71, his bride being 40."[3] Leslie left San Francisco in 1906, following the earthquake and fire, and moved to Berkeley, on the east shore of San Francisco Bay. He would remain in Berkeley until 1914.

John Ralph Dean continued with his self-aggrandizement during a visit to Tucson on March 1, 1907. As usual, Dean quickly found a reporter who would write up his real and imagined exploits. Once again, Buckskin Frank Leslie would be a character in the latest version of Arizona history that Dean decided to spin: "J. R. Dean, an Arizonian of many years pioneer life, is in the city representing the Omaha Hotel Supply company, in which he is financially interested. Johnny Dean, as he was popularly known, and Frank Leslie are historic characters of Arizona." This much we can accept as accurate. Dean continued in describing himself and Leslie as "noted Indian scouts under both General Crook and General

Miles [who] operated together in the field and were as brothers at home and on scouting expeditions." He and Leslie "were with General Lawton when he made his famous pursuit of Chief Geronimo and his Apache tigers and were always in the lead." Still, according to Dean, they "were present at the surrender of Geronimo and his treacherous Apache tribe to General Miles." These two were "two of the bravest men and truest friends to their friends and ever to the front in the perilous days of the Arizona Apache wars, and during the time when outlaws made Arizona their hiding place, committing many deeds of violence." He continued:

> Both were quiet and unobtrusive, mild as two Quaker boys, but when occasion came for action were as quick as a flash. Both were dead shots. The headquarters of these frontiersmen was at Tombstone during the bloody period of that silver camp. They were always on the side of law and order, and rendered invaluable service in the days of tribulation and struggle for civilization.

Dean of course could not have envisioned anyone even questioning his statements. He continued, describing himself and Leslie as "frontier heroes" who were engaged in "prosperous business." Johnny Dean represented the Omaha Hotel Supply Company, and Frank Leslie was the "secretary of a prosperous mining company with an office in Oakland, Cal."[4]

The following year, during March 1908, Dean, now calling himself "Major J.R. Dean of Seattle," was visiting Texas and was interviewed by a reporter from the *Houston Post.* Dean's recollections of his past and the celebrated people he supposedly knew grew more improbable with each passing year. In this 1908 *Houston Post* interview, Dean claimed to have been "personally acquainted" with no less a figure than Billy the Kid. Dean also claimed to have known Pat Garrett. Of course, the Kid and Garrett were being used in the *Houston Post* interview as an excuse for Dean to once again spin a yarn about a frontier celebrity he actually did know: "Buckskin Frank" Leslie:

> Major J.R. Dean of Seattle, Wash., who is a guest at the Hotel Brazos, was a ranchman in New Mexico in the early eighties, and knew Pat Garrett, who while sheriff of that county, killed "Billy the Kid," who had a record of having killed more than twenty men. Mr. Dean was also personally acquainted with "Billy the Kid," whom he declares was not a bad sort of fellow. . . .
>
> "After the death of 'Billy the Kid,' a young chap named Billy Claiborne wanted to emulate the example of the desperado, and called himself 'Billy the Kid, No. 2.' After he served a term in the penitentiary, he came back, and in order to make a reputation as a killer, started after Frank Leslie, known as 'Buckskin Frank,' who was a partner of mine in the cattle business, was a college graduate and one of the most polished men I ever met. He is now secretary of a big mining company. 'Billy the Kid No. 2,' took one shot at Leslie. The bullet grazed the latter's ear, and then with one shot he ended the existence of the would-be desperado. 'Buckskin Frank' apologized to Claiborne because he was forced to shoot him, and was the only mourner at his funeral.
>
> "The only really bad men in those days were the would-be bad men. Unoffending strangers were never attacked by the really brave men of those stirring days on the frontier. I remember once seeing 'Buckskin Frank' slap the face of a cowboy, who shot off the hat of 'Boss' Pike, then a traveling man, but now a large jobber in Frisco."[5]

James B. Neal was back in the news when he shot George Mulkey at the Westfall Ranch in Cochise County on June 12, 1908. Mulkey died from his wounds the next day. In their coverage of the killing, the *Bisbee Daily Review* included a report of how the fifty-year-old Neal had once, himself, been the victim of a shooting:

> The recent shooting and subsequent death of Mulkey at the hands of Neal, recalls a shooting scrape that happened several years ago at the Leslie ranch in the Swisshelm Mountains, in which Neal was a party, but in that instance was the man shot. Neal and a

> woman were at the ranch of Frank Leslie, Leslie living with the woman, and Neal being employed there. Leslie came home one night and finding the parties together, drew his six-shooter and shot the woman, killing her almost instantly, and then fired four shots into the body of Neal, and left him for dead. Leslie then came into Tombstone and gave himself up, stating that he had killed the two parties, but had done so in self-defense.
>
> Had that been the fact he would have escaped being sent to Yuma, for there would have been no one to dispute his story as there were no other witnesses to the shooting. But he had not killed Neal.
>
> Neal, after being unconscious for several hours after he was shot, regained his senses and crawled on his hands and knees a distance of three miles to an adjoining ranch where he was temporarily taken care of until he could be brought to town for medical treatment. Leslie was indicted and convicted of killing the woman on the testimony given by Neal. He served a term of ten years. Leslie was a noted frontiersman and army scout and had been in the west a number of years. He is now in Alaska. [6]

Despite the claim by the *Bisbee Daily Review* that Leslie was "now in Alaska," there is absolutely no evidence that Leslie ever set foot in Alaska. At the time this article was published in the Bisbee newspaper, Leslie was living at 1348 Shattuck Avenue in Berkeley, California.

James Wilson Orndorff was the subject of an article revealing that he had originated an expression that later became a staple of pulp westerns, as well as of Hollywood "oaters." During July 1908, the *San Diego Union* noted that "twenty years ago in San Francisco, the term 'tin horn gambler' was attributed to Hon. James Orndorff who was dealing in a gambling place on the Comstock lode. It was said that he remarked to a player at the game who was playing small: 'You're cheaper than a tin horn.' When the question was referred to Orndorff for settlement he replied: 'Pears to me I did say something like that, anyhow that's what he was, he was nothing but a tin horn.'"[7]

The city directory listings for Berkeley, California, were part of a separate section of the *Oakland City Directory.* Leslie was listed as "Frank N. Leslie, " living at 1348 Shattuck Avenue in Berkeley in the 1908 directory (1352), and was listed as a being a "miner." The 1909 city directory (1106) listed him at the same address, but gave his correct name as "N. Frank Leslie," and his occupation as "mining."

Early in 1910, Leslie moved to 2918 Ellsworth Street in Berkeley, a home recently purchased by a thirty-eight-year-old widow with two young children. The 1910 United States Federal Census for Berkeley listed the occupants of this home as being a forty-year-old widow named Clara Younkins, living with her two young children, a son named James N., age seven, and a daughter named Gladys, five years old. Also listed as being part of this household was "Frank Leslie, age 65" (he was actually sixty-eight), who gave his birthplace as "Texas," and was also described as being "widowed." According to this 1910 Alameda County census, Leslie's occupation was a "servant" in Clara Taylor Younkins's household.[8]

As might be expected, Leslie's actual role in the widow Younkins's household was a little more involved than simply being a "servant." This is not to suggest anything of a sexual nature existed between them. The real attraction was something they both had in common—mining.

Clara Taylor was twenty-nine years old when she married a forty-three-year-old mine owner named James Buchannan Younkins on January 15, 1900, in Dawson City, Yukon, Canada. Their two children were born in Dawson City: Gladys Fern Younkins on April 27, 1904, and James North Younkins on July 9, 1905. Clara's husband, James Buchannan Younkins, was only fifty-two when he died in Dawson City on August 17, 1909. His estate consisted of valuable mining property in the Dawson City area, including, but not limited to, the not so imaginatively named "Last Chance Mine."

Why Clara decided to settle in Berkeley, California, soon after her husband's death isn't known. What is known is that it didn't take Leslie long to find out about her arrival and to move in with her and her children at 2918 Ellsworth Street. Clara might have been attracted by the fact that Leslie looked enough like her late husband to be taken for an older brother. His real appeal would have been his mining expertise, which dated back at least thirty years by the time they met, as well as his ability to offer his advice on the various gold-producing properties she still held title to in Dawson City. We don't know exactly how long Leslie remained part of this household. He lived there for at least a year, and was listed as "N. Frank Leslie" at that address in the 1911 city directory for Berkeley.

The sixty-nine-year-old Leslie either dismissed thoughts of proposing marriage to the widow Younkins, or perhaps had been rejected if he actually did propose. His seventy-eight-year-old friend, James Wilson Orndorff, was having better luck. The twice-widowed Orndorff decided to try his luck one final time when he married his housekeeper, Helen J. "Nellie" Battis, who was fifty-six. They were married on November 12, 1912, in San Rafael, California. Perhaps encouraged by Orndoff's success, Leslie would soon meet a new woman and elect to try marriage again.

Chapter 15

Marriage to Elnora Torbert Cast

Elnora Torbert Cast was the third woman whom Leslie would legally marry and the third who had been married previously. She was born on December 24, 1868, in Milford, Illinois. Her name at birth was Elnora Torbert, but she preferred to be called "Nora." Her first husband was Elmer A. Cast (1868–1924). They were married in Iroquois, Illinois, on September 21, 1889, and would become the parents of six children born between 1890 and 1903. The couple was living in Wenatchee, Washington, on May 18, 1908, when the local paper reported their divorce.[1]

Nora was living in Napa, California, when she met Leslie. They were married by a Justice of the Peace in Napa on November 6, 1913. On their marriage certificate, Leslie gave his birthplace as Texas, and his occupation as "miner." More importantly, Leslie identified his parents by name on this certificate. He wrote that his father was "Bernard Leslie," who was born in Virginia, and that his mother was "Martha Leslie," whose birthplace was Kentucky. It is still not known how truthful Leslie was in regard to the names of his parents, and their birthplaces; these two individuals have not been located on the respective censuses. He certainly wasn't truthful when he gave his age as being fifty-four on the certificate, when he was actually seventy-one. Nora, for her part, wrote her actual age of forty-three on the document. She would turn forty-four the following month.[2]

The new Mrs. Leslie was crazy about Washington State where she had resided for a few years before she and Elmer A. Cast divorced. Nora Leslie managed to talk her new husband into checking out the state—particularly a small town called Omak. Leslie agreed and they took a trip there during March 1914. According to the local paper, "Capt. N.F. Leslie, of Berkeley, California arrived in Omak Monday [March 2, 1914] and may decide to locate here permanently. Mr. Leslie became interested in this country through his recent marriage to the former Mrs. Nora Cast."[3] It is known that they moved to Omak, Washington, and that Nora would remain there until her dying day. Leslie remained there just a little over two years.

By May 7, 1915, it had been nearly thirty-five years since the shooting of Mike Killeen in Tombstone on the porch of the Bilicke family's Cosmopolitan Hotel. It happened on a date which also happened to be Albert Clay Bilicke's nineteenth birthday. By May 7, 1915, Albert Clay Bilicke was a multi-millionaire. In 1915 dollars his wealth was estimated at $2,000,000—the equivalent of nearly $47,000,000 when adjusted to 2017 dollars. On May 7, 1915, Albert Clay Bilicke and his wife were in their stateroom on the *Lusitania*, when the ship was torpedoed by the German U-boat *U-20* off the coast of Ireland. Albert Clay Bilicke was one of the 1,198 people who were killed. His wife, Gladys Huff Bilicke, was one of the 761 who survived. She provided an account of the tragedy a few weeks later. The *San Francisco Chronicle* picked up the story from Los Angeles, dateline June 4. It relates the facts of how Albert Clay Bilicke perished, but the words could not convey the tragic aspect of his passing. His widow told how it happened to a friend who in turn passed it on anonymously to the Los Angeles source. Mrs. Bilicke who was named as one of the executors of her husband's $2,000,000 estate, was then in

New York, on her way home. "My husband and I were in our stateroom when the first torpedo struck. . . . We rushed upon the deck. The boats were being lowered and we took our places in one. There were about fifty persons in the boat and before it reached the water it shot down suddenly and plunged beneath the water, carrying us all with it." At that point everyone may have believed they had no hope, but some struggled to survive a few more minutes. She recalled, "Mr. Bilicke never came up. I fought my way to the surface. It seemed hours before I came up near a floating spar or piece of timber. Several men were clinging to it and one helped me obtain a hold. Hours passed and with them one man after another muttered 'Good-by' and dropped back into the water, until not one remained." Mrs. Bilicke did not mention the idea that God was instrumental in saving her, but offered this reason for her survival: "But I believe I was possessed of superhuman strength and held on for four hours until I was picked up."[4]

Albert Clay Bilicke was possibly the wealthiest of all the rich men who had played a part in Leslie's life. As a nineteen-year-old in Tombstone, Albert had not yet acquired the fabulous wealth that would be his at the time of his death. Yet, in 1880, despite still being a teenager, he was an equal partner with his father in Tombstone's Cosmopolitan Hotel, as well as other properties. Leslie's relationship with other wealthy men, such as Milton E. Joyce and James Wilson Orndorff, has been detailed throughout this book. He was comfortable being around rich men, who sought out his company. These relationships raise the question of Leslie's own wealth.

From November 1881 when Leslie owned and operated two separate saloons, across the street from each other in Tombstone, until the spring of 1916, there is no evidence showing that Leslie had ever experienced financial difficulties. He always seemed to land on his feet, even after serving a prison term at Yuma. This is not to suggest that Leslie was rich, but he always seemed to have whatever cash he needed to go wherever he wanted to go.

Leslie's various mining interests, most of which were in Mexico, were the likely source of his unexplained income. At the age of seventy-four, Leslie left Omak, Washington, and his wife Nora, for what is believed to have been the last time. He was headed back to Sonora, Mexico, to check on mining interests he had there. On his way to Mexico, Leslie was interviewed by a *Seattle Daily Times* reporter on May 20, 1916:

> BUCKSKIN FRANK TO BRAVE YAQUIS IN OLD MEXICO
>
> Plainsman and Army Scout, Capt. N. Frank Leslie,
>
> En Route for a Dash to Look at Mine Property.
>
> Resolved to brave the dangers of the Sonora mining district, despite the known antagonism of the part-Yaqui inhabitants of that section of Mexico, Capt. N. Frank Leslie, plainsman and army scout, is in Seattle en route to join three other adventurous ones at Naco, Ariz., preparatory to making a dash to the properties of the El Rey del Oro Mining Company in southern Sonora near the near the Chihuahua border.
>
> Captain Leslie, known throughout the great Southwest as "Buckskin Frank," was chief of the band of scouts which led a force of regulars under Capt. H.W. Lawton, later a general, to the hiding place of the Indian chief, Geronimo, in his last expedition. He also acted as chief of scouts under Generals Crook and Miles. During his years of service with the United States army he was wounded on several occasions, suffered terrible hardships, and emerged with his life and the most remarkable knowledge of the Arizona, New Mexico, Southern Nevada and Northern Mexico country possessed by any man living today, according to regular army officers.
>
> Going to Look Over Property.
>
> "We are going in to look over our property," said Captain Leslie yesterday, "always provided we can get to it. Letters received

today indicate that the Carranzistas have the upper hand in that district now and that Americans are not as badly hated as was the case a few weeks ago.

"Of course the dislike of the Gringo is inborn in most Mexicans, and because of that condition we may encounter difficulties on our trip. There will be but four of us in two motor cars, as it is probable a small force will be better proof of peaceful intent than if our force was in the nature of an expedition of a score or more. We will go prepared for our own protection, of course.

"The company's mine is a rich gold producer in the heart of a rich copper country. The greatest difficulty with the fields at present, particularly for copper, is the lack of coke for smelting purposes. It may not be possible to go ahead with work until the country is pacified, but on the other hand we are anxious to know the condition of our buildings and machinery. If anything is left and Mexican conditions quiet down we should be in operation again before fall."[5]

The article from the *Seattle Times* of May 20, 1916, is the last time that we can place Leslie in an exact location until 1920. We don't know if he actually got to Mexico and, if he did, how long he stayed there. There is no known record of him returning to his wife in Omak, Washington. If they didn't actually divorce, Leslie and Nora had clearly separated by 1920, when he was recorded on the United States Federal Census as being a resident of Sausalito, California.

May Killeen Leslie Durward's third husband was remembered in Tombstone on October 14, 1917, when the *Epitaph* reported that "Alexander Durward, who was connected with the Cochise Hardware and Trading Company in Tombstone in its early days, and who is well known to many residents, and who has been in the lumber business at Yuma for a number of years, has disposed of his interests there. He also has extensive interests at Banning, California. He was married in Tombstone a number of years ago to Mrs. Frank Leslie."[6]

On January 27, 1920, the United States Federal Census enumerator Harry J. Thomas recorded that Leslie was living at 959 Water Street in Sausalito, California, where he was described as a seventy-seven-year-old lodger who was "single." He was living in a home owned by James W. Orndorff, age eighty-five, and his wife Helen Jane "Nellie" Orndorff, age sixty-three. On that 1920 census, James W. Orndorff was listed as "Proprietor of Pool and Billiard Parlor" in Sausalito. That January 27, 1920, census for Sausalito, California, is the final record we have for Leslie while he was still alive.[7]

Some might conclude that Leslie was down and out, and that a wealthy friend had taken him into his home as an act of charity—but there is no evidence that this was the case in 1920. It is more likely that the two men were drawn together, in their old age, because of the many things they had in common. James Wilson Orndorff had started out as a miner when he arrived in Virginia City, Nevada, in 1863. By the time he left Virginia City in 1880 he owned several mining properties there, as well as a hotel, a saloon, and the first of his many billiard halls. Like Orndorff, Leslie had extensive mining experience and owned a couple of saloons in Tombstone during his early years there.

In his younger days, Orndorff had been a billiard champion and he never lost interest in the game. Having the seventy-seven-year-old Leslie as a "lodger" in his home would have given the eighty-five-year-old Orndorff someone he could play billiards with on a regular basis. A plus for Orndorff would have been having someone around who was as knowledgeable about mining as he was. Both men had been notable figures in two of the wildest towns of the Wild West: Virginia City and Tombstone. Orndorff may have had the edge in wealth, but in every other respect they were evenly matched. Leslie and Ordndorff would have been too old in 1920 to go prospecting and to locate new mining claims, but it is probable that they grubstaked others.

During April 1921, a Phoenix newspaper called the *Arizona Republican* published an interview with George A. Mauk headlined "Life in

Tombstone When Place was the Wildest and Wooliest in the West." The *Arizona Republican* described Mauk as "himself a pioneer of that district. Mr. Mauk, now of Phoenix, first went to Tombstone in 1880, and has been a resident of Arizona since." Mauk gave his reminiscences of several noted Tombstone characters. In remembering Leslie, Mauk informed the *Republican* that he "gave his name as Frank Leslie, but through the years his identity has never been established." This does suggest that Nashville Franklyn Leslie may not have been his real name. But presumably Mauk knew Leslie well, adding that Leslie "was from a good family and presumably had a college education. To all appearances, Buckskin Frank was a man of a delicate nature, but he soon established a reputation that made him one of the most feared men in the Tombstone district. . . . Only a few years ago Leslie was seen in San Francisco, where he was a member of the Union League. He was a special body guard to [Rudolph] Spreckels and Francis Heney during the trial of Abe Ruff [*sic*] and Mayor Schmidt [*sic*] on charges of graft and corruption."[8]

The first interesting question Mauk's account raises concerns Leslie's being a member of San Francisco's Union Club—which would have been a strange choice for a man who claimed to have worn the Confederate gray.[9] Mauk describes Leslie as being a "bodyguard" for Mayor Eugene Schmitz (1864-1928) of San Francisco "a few years ago," during the trial of Schmitz and Abraham Ruef (1864-1936), which actually concluded with Schmitz being removed from office on June 13, 1907, nearly fourteen years earlier, rather than a "few years." What makes Mauk's account interesting is the mention of Francis Joseph Heney (1859-1937) who had been a Tucson resident during the time that Leslie was active in and around Tombstone.[10]

The third, and final, husband of May Killeen Leslie Durward died in Banning, California, on September 27, 1922, at the age of 68. Durward was still remembered well in Tombstone; the *Tombstone Weekly Epitaph* paid a tribute to him: "Alexander Durward, for 13 years the owner of the Colorado River Lumber Company in Yuma, died Wednesday morning at his home in Banning, Calif., according to a message received yesterday from D.A. Innes." Durward was born in Scotland, January 11, 1854. After his arrival in the United States at the age of twenty-one he spent "the remainder of his life in the building of the great Southwest." Durward was well known among the old timers of Tombstone. After coming to Cochise County in the early eighties he was engaged in the freighting business, driving one of the big eighteen-mule teams into Bisbee, hauling coke and other supplies to the smelters from Benson. He later drove from Tombstone to the various mills that were located along the San Pedro River at Charlestown, Grand Central, and Contention. The laudatory obituary continued:

> He quit the freighting business and was for a few years connected with the Cochise Hardware and Trading Company in Tombstone. He left Tombstone a number of years ago and went to Yuma, where he engaged in the lumber business and then moved to Banning, California, where he was engaged in the lumber business.
>
> While in Tombstone he married Mrs. Frank Leslie, who had secured a divorce from Leslie. Leslie was one of the well-known characters of the early days of Tombstone.[11]

James Wilson Orndorff, Leslie's longtime friend, died on February 16, 1923, at the age of eighty-eight. Orndorff owned several properties in various California locations. At the time of his death, Orndorff was living at 130 Pierce Street in San Francisco. Whether the eighty-year-old Leslie was still a "lodger" at Orndorff's other property, at 959 Water Street in Sausalito, remains unknown.

There is one final document, in which Leslie's other longtime friend, John Ralph Dean, described Leslie as still being alive as late as September 9, 1923. On that date, Dean wrote the actor William S. Hart advising him to contact "Capt. N.F. Leslie" in care of "Orndorff's Billiard Parlors, Berkeley, Calif." Hart was then making a film called *Wild Bill Hickok*, and Dean, who signed the letter "Lt. Col. John R. Dean," recommended Leslie as a technical advisor. Dean described Leslie as "my old time pard who was considered the quickest man with a gun in all of Arizona and Texas. You may have heard of him, Frank Leslie, better known as Buckskin Frank. He was a partner of Wild Bill's in Abilene, Kansas and when Bill was Marshal Leslie was his chief deputy. Leslie is living in Berkeley, Calif. and if you want some straight facts you can get it from him, Capt. N. Frank Leslie."[12]

No record has been found showing that William S. Hart succeeded in contacting Leslie. It probably didn't help that John Ralph Dean gave the location of "Orndorff's Billiard Parlors" as being in Berkeley, which is in Alameda County, rather than the actual location of Sausalito, in Marin County. Hart's search (if he made one) would have been further complicated by the fact that James W. Orndorff had died more than six months before Dean wrote his letter to Hart. It does seem likely that Hart would have attempted to track Leslie down, since the actor was well known for forming friendships with Wild West figures such as Bat Masterson and Wyatt Earp.[13]

Chapter 16

The Death of Buckskin Frank Leslie

The celebrated actress Lotta Crabtree had died in Boston on September 25, 1924, leaving an estate valued at $4,000,000. She had no known surviving heirs—but that didn't stop a large number of people from claiming a relationship to get a share of the fortune. All but one were eliminated until it finally came down to forty-five-year-old Mrs. Carlotta Cockburn, who as an eight-month-old baby, had been left by her mother with Frank and May Leslie back in 1881. She had been born as Carlotta Crabtree, adopted by Ed Bullock and raised as Carlotta Bullock before marrying a man named Cockburn.

The court proceedings over Carlotta's claim began in Boston on December 3, 1926. A California newspaper reported that "Mrs. Carlotta Cockburn of San Gabriel, California, today began in the Suffolk Probate Court here, her fight to establish herself as the daughter of Jack Crabtree and therefore entitled to share in the four million dollar estate left by her aunt, Lotta Crabtree, actress."[1] Seventy-year-old May Killeen Leslie Durward gave her testimony on December 7, 1926, when it was reported that "Mrs. Deerwood [*sic*], in whose care the baby was left when the mother was seeking Crabtree, began her story at the time she was the wife of Mike Killeen. Mike, she said started shooting at her, and one of his bullets struck 'Buckskin Frank' Leslie. So 'Buckskin Frank' began shooting and he killed Mike Killeen. Then she married 'Buckskin Frank,' but later got a divorce." [2]

On March 31, 1927, the "right of Carlotta Cockburn of San Gabriel, California to contest the will of Lotta Crabtree, Boston actress, who left a $4,000,000 estate to charity, was denied by Judge [William M.] Prest of the Suffolk Probate Court. Mrs. Cockburn claimed that she was the daughter of John A. Crabtree, brother of Lotta, and therefore an heir.... The judge found that there was no ceremonial marriage between Jack Crabtree and Annie Leopold, parents of the petitioner, as Mrs. Cockburn had claimed."[3] The decision was appealed to the Massachusetts Supreme Court who affirmed the judgment of the probate court judge on June 14, 1928, effectively ending any additional court appearances by Carlotta Cockburn as a claimant to the $4,000,000 Lotta Crabtree estate.

Whatever memories of "Buckskin Frank" came over Mrs. Durward during this period must remain speculative, but for other Tombstone citizens certainly people could gather and talk about the days when Tombstone was the mecca for so many adventure seekers. The interest in Buckskin Frank Leslie may have dimmed for some, but it continued when a new type of historian entered upon the scene, the kind who insisted on grass-level research and documenting their claims. No matter that Walter Noble Burns or Stuart N. Lake found financial success in their writings; some readers and researchers were compelled to find the accurate story. One of these was Philip J. Rasch.

In 1954 researcher Philip J. Rasch published a sixteen-page article called "A Note on Buckskin Frank Leslie," in which he said he was told "that an individual named Charles Valero, described as an importer in El Paso, claimed to be Leslie's son by a Mexican woman and to possess his diary. It is said that he alleges that Leslie died in Los Angeles on August 24, 1924. Neither the City of Los Angeles nor the State of California possesses any record of Leslie's death and Valero himself is completely unknown to the importing fraternity in El Paso."[4]

The authors of this book decided to look into Rasch's 1954 claim by "Charles Valero" that "Leslie died in Los Angeles on August 24, 1924." In fact *three* separate men named "Frank Leslie" died in Los Angeles in 1924—on April 1, April 8, and June 26. The *Los Angeles Times* provided very short death notices for the three men named "Frank Leslie." The first "Frank Leslie," who died on April 1, 1924, can be eliminated since he was described as being fifty-six-years-old.[5] No age was given for the second "Frank Leslie" who died on April 8, and was taken to the same funeral home.[6] The most details were provided for the third "Frank Leslie," who died on June 26, 1924—although no age was given for the deceased.[7]

Leslie's 1999 biographer, Don Chaput, related the story of how Leslie, circa 1924, was "one of the old Tombstone crowd who had gravitated to the Bay area. The center for much of this gathering was the book store of Alec Robertson, facing Union Square. Robertson had a variety of jobs in early Tombstone, including that of deputy sheriff."[8] Leslie, supposedly a regular visitor at Alec Robertson's bookstore, suddenly stopped coming. Robertson became concerned and went to a billiard hall in Oakland, where Leslie also spent a lot of his time, and did occasional odd jobs. Years later, Alec Robertson told historian Robert Mullin what the owner of the Oakland billiard hall said, which was then shared with Earp's biographer, Stuart N. Lake. Although the report came third hand, apparently Leslie had "walked out of the place one day and simply had not returned; he had just been paid a few dollars coming to him, and after his departure, the proprietor missed a pistol which he kept out of sight back of the cash register." Alec recalled that on his last visit to the store, Frank had been "unusually low, physically and mentally. A search was made of hospitals, morgues and hospital records, in several counties, but no trace of Frank. His friends feared that he had sought some secluded spot in the hills and used the gun to end it all."[9]

The story that Leslie used a pistol, stolen from a pool room, to commit suicide in a remote California location would be repeated time and again in the years that followed. Then, an event seemingly unconnected to Leslie would cast serious doubt on all those claims that Leslie had died by his own hand. It began on August 19, 1925, when an Oakland, California, nurse named Bessie Ferguson Loren disappeared. There is no evidence that the Oakland nurse and Frank Leslie ever met in life, but, they will always be linked by their deaths, which happened in the same location only twenty-four months apart. Neither Leslie nor the nurse died from natural causes, as this article from the September 9, 1925, issue of the *San Bernardino Daily Sun* illustrates:

Locate More Murder Bones.

Hunting Cap and Surgeon's Tubing
Also Located in Swamp Death Probe.

> OAKLAND, Sept. 8—Bay Farm Island gave up further gruesome evidence in the murder and mutilation of Bessie Ferguson Loren today when searchers in the grass and weed grown marshes along the shores came upon all of the missing bones of the sawed up skeleton excepting the hands and feet.
>
> The discovery was made by J.W. Gomez and Floyd Kennedy, Oakland youths, who yesterday found other missing bones and other evidence. Near the bones found today were a man's hunting cap and sections of rubber tubing such as surgeons use. Officials are hopeful that the cap and the pair of trousers and coat found yesterday may aid in the discovery of the slayer or slayers. A portion of human lung with a section of windpipe was turned over to officials today by J.W. Baldwin of Oakland.
>
> Dr. O.D. Hamlin of Oakland today set about reconstructing the skeleton of the slain nurse. Nearly every bone recovered so far has

> been sawed into fragments, making the reconstruction a tedious process.
>
> Sheriff R.R. Veale of *Contra Costa County* [authors' italics], said today that he would call for an inquest at which every person whose name has been brought into the case would be required to testify, under oath.[10]

William A. Mills, a researcher from Perry, Georgia, has located evidence showing that eighty-four-year-old Nashville Franklyn Leslie was still alive as late as October 15, 1926. The following day *The Morning Oregonian* included the name "N.F. Leslie" as part of a lengthy passenger list of the *Rose City*, a steamer departing Portland bound for San Francisco. We know that this particular "N.F. Leslie" was a man, since women and girls were always identified on passenger lists with a "Miss" or "Mrs." preceding their names. Men and boys were identified by their names alone. [11]

In 1961 a writer named Tom Bailey wrote a magazine article in which he added a few more details to the story of Leslie stealing a gun from an Oakland billiard hall. According to Bailey, the proprietor reported the gun stolen to the police and provided them with the weapon's serial number. Bailey claimed that a body was found, some three years later, in a canyon north of Martinez, California. Bailey claimed that a revolver was found next to the body, and that the Martinez and Oakland police traced it to the billiard hall where Leslie was last seen.[12]

The Bailey article has been roundly dismissed by historians, since it contained several factual errors. Bailey claimed that he had interviewed Leslie in 1911, and that Leslie disappeared with the stolen pistol shortly afterward. Bailey then went on to say that the body and stolen pistol were found in that "canyon north of Martinez, California," three years later—meaning 1914, when documents show that Leslie was very much alive. It now turns out that, despite being off by several years on his timeline, Tom Bailey may, in fact, have been pointing us in the right direction after all.

On December 1, 2016, the authors of this book received an early Christmas present from researcher William A. Mills, in the form of an article he found in a California newspaper called the *Healdsburg Tribune* that was published on November 2, 1927. This article offers the earliest account of Frank Leslie's death. Leslie obviously, as the account will show, did not die by his own hand nor in a blazing gunfight, but was a murder victim. The italics are by the authors of this book:

BONES FOUND IN PIT DISCLOSE
A POSSIBLE MURDER

SKELETON LOCATED NEAR SPOT WHERE OAKLAND NURSE WAS SLAIN

> MARTINEZ, Nov. 2—Charred human bones, including the skull, police say, of *an elderly man* were found Monday [October 31, 1927] afternoon in a shallow pit on the west slope of Tapscott hill in El Cerrito, Contra Costa county.
>
> The find of the skeleton of *another possible murder victim* was made near the tule swamp where the dismembered body of Mrs. Bessie Ferguson Loren, Oakland nurse, was hidden two years ago [1925] last August.
>
> Henry Marco, a baker, 1568 Curtiss Street, El Cerrito, made the discovery walking in the northern part of the town, near the Richmond city boundary. He had kicked up loose dirt when traversing the *marshy pit* and he saw part of a bone projecting from the ground. After a little prodding the grave gave up almost a complete skeleton and the uppers and heels of a *number seven pair of shoes.* There were buttons, apparently all that was left of a pair of overalls.
>
> The coroner of Contra Costa county said the bones undoubtedly were those of *an elderly man about five feet seven inches in height*

> and of a heavy build. A copy of a *Seattle newspaper*, issue of October 5, was found near the exhibit.[13]

There is no question that the skeleton found on October 31, 1927, was that of Nashville Franklyn "Buckskin Frank" Leslie. His remains were found in El Cerrito, Contra Costa County, California, which was, not surprisingly, part of the San Francisco Bay Area.[14] What is surprising is that all the available evidence points to Leslie being murdered—perhaps by a serial killer. The description of what remained of his charred skeleton matches Leslie perfectly. We know from his 1890 prison records that Leslie was 5 feet 7 ¼ inches and wore a size 5 boot at the time he entered Yuma. The murder victim found in 1927 wore a size 7 shoe. There are reasons that can be given for the discrepancy in the 1890 size 5 boot size and the 1927 shoe size. The most plausible is that Leslie, as often happens with men as they age, then and now, found he was comfortable wearing a larger shoe size. Going from a size 5 to a size 7 was not a huge difference, given that thirty-seven years had passed. It is also noteworthy that the size 5 boot or size 7 shoe was very small for a man of Leslie's height. There is certainly no question that, at the age of eighty-five, Leslie would have fit the description of an "elderly man" at the time of his 1927 murder.

On the same day that the *Healdsburg Tribune* article appeared, the *San Francisco Chronicle* of November 2, 1927, published this very similar, but far more detailed, article. The article contained a couple of minor errors, which were overshadowed by the significant information that was not found in the *Healdsburg Tribune* version:

> Skeleton Reveals Murder of
> Mysterious Stranger
>
> Charred human bones, including the skull, police say, of an elderly man were found yesterday [*sic*] afternoon on the west slope of Tapscott hill in El Cerrito, Contra Costa County. The find of the skeleton of another possible murder victim was made near the

> tule swamp where the dismembered body of Mrs. Bessie Ferguson Loren, Oakland nurse, was hidden two years ago [1925] last August.
>
> Henry Marco, a baker, 1503 [*sic*] Curtiss Street, El Cerrito, made the discovery when walking in the northern part of the town, near the Richmond city boundary. He had kicked up loose dirt when traversing the marshy pit and he saw part of a bone projecting from the ground. After a little prodding, the grave gave up almost a complete skeleton and the uppers and heels of a number seven pair of shoes. There also were buttons, apparently all that was left of a pair of overalls.
>
> El Cerrito police believe the body was burned soon after death, as there were no signs of decay. They expressed the belief that gasoline had been used. Coroner Aubrey Wilson of Contra Costa County last night took charge of the bones at the scene, while the sheriff's office and police of the bay cities joined in solving the mystery.
>
> The coroner said that the bones undoubtedly were those of an elderly man of about five feet seven inches in height and of a heavy build. According to Deputy Coroner George Reifschneider, the body had been buried two months. Sheriff's officers have turned over to E.O. Heinrich, Berkeley criminologist, for examination, a piece of silk hat band, a portion of a shoe and parts of teeth, found with the bones.[15]

Although the *San Francisco Chronicle* article was far more detailed than the similar *Healdsburg Tribune* version, it did not contain any mention of the October 5, 1927, Seattle newspaper found with Leslie's bones. The newspaper's date challenges the deputy coroner's assertion that "the body had been buried two months," which suggested a death date of early September 1927. Coroner Aubrey Wilson's description of Leslie having "a heavy build" is also interesting. How Coroner Wilson came to that conclusion, from a badly burned skeleton, remains unclear. Leslie was consistently described as being slim, well into his fifties. It could very well have been that, as an "elderly man" of eighty-five, Leslie had packed on extra pounds due to age and inactivity.

The story was picked up by out-of-state newspapers, including the *Bellingham Herald*, from the state of Washington, which shed more light on the October 5, 1927, issue of the Seattle newspaper. The italics are by the authors of this book.

> Murder Clues Slim.
>
> El CERRITO, CAL., Nov. 3—Two strands of blonde hair and a copy of the *Seattle Times*, dated October 5, 1927, were the only clues uncovered today by officers investigating the discovery of charred human bones found near here Tuesday. *Both the paper and the hair were in the grave beneath the bones.* Crime experts last night declared the bones seemed to be those of a middle-aged man and said *the flesh had been burned away either with acid or a blowtorch.* The bones were found by Henry Marco, who is here visiting a sister, Mrs. John Curtis. Almost a complete skeleton was assembled. The *skull was fractured*, but whether the fracture occurred before or after death remains to be determined.
>
> Auto Seen Near Grave
>
> The proprietor of a service station within sight of the *shallow grave* where the bones were found, told police that he had seen an automobile parked near the grave Friday [October 28, 1927] night. A deputy coroner [George Reifschneider] estimated that *the body had been buried about a month.* But detectives surmised that whoever buried the bones might have returned to learn whether they had been discovered. One theory advanced by the police was that *the victim might have been murdered elsewhere* and brought here for burial.

Much to be Learned

> All clues were turned over to E.O. Heinrich, Berkeley criminologist, and police hoped that by tomorrow [November 4, 1927] he will have determined whether the bones are those of a small man, a woman or youth. All these classifications were made by investigators, although examination of the jawbone, vertebrae and teeth were said to support the statement that the victim was a man.[16]

Of all the criminal investigators then living in 1927 California, it would have been difficult to find anyone who was more qualified to lead an investigation of the skeleton found in El Cerrito, than forty-six-year-old "E.O. Heinrich, Berkeley criminologist." He was celebrated throughout the state as being the "Edison of Crime Detection." Unlike the real Edison, who forever changed the way the world was illuminated, Heinrich shed no light on the skeleton found in El Cerrito, and ultimately proved himself to be a dim bulb in this particular investigation.[17]

A new wrinkle was added on November 5, 1927, when Police Chief Daniel Cox of Richmond, California received an "anonymous" communication from a person who thought he witnessed the cremation that resulted in a charred skeleton. The following day, the *Oakland Tribune* gave this report:

Mystery Killing Linked by Letter to Fire on Hill

> RICHMOND, Nov. 5 – An anonymous letter received by Police Chief Daniel Cox of this city tells that its writer saw a fire on Tapscott hill in El Cerrito, where a charred skeleton was found this week. The incident occurred *six months ago*, the letter states. It is the belief of local authorities that there is no significance to the report, as the exposed position of the human remains would have caused their discovery before six months had elapsed.
>
> Effort is being made, however, by Chief Cox to ascertain the identity of the writer of the communication, in order that further information may be elicited. The letter told that but one man was

> tending the blaze. It has been the opinion of investigators that the body was destroyed by some powerful chemical agent or a gasoline blowtorch.[18]

Given his otherwise stellar reputation as a criminologist, it is difficult to explain how E.O. Heinrich could come to the conclusion that Leslie had "dropped dead" while out for a hike, and that his severely burned skeleton was the result of a "grass fire." Heinrich's findings completely ignored the fact that Leslie's scorched skeleton had been buried, and that his skull had been fractured. Deputy Coroner George Reifschneider of Richmond, California responded with "complete disbelief" at Heinrich's conclusions, according to the *Oakland Tribune*:

> Coroner, Heinrich Differ on Skeleton
>
> RICHMOND, Nov. 9 —Complete disbelief in the theory of E.O. Heinrich, Berkeley criminologist, that the charred skeleton found last week in El Cerrito bore evidence of natural death and incineration in a grass fire, is expressed by Deputy Coroner George Reifschneider of this city. The body is that of a man murdered and consumed by a powerful heat agent, he feels certain. He concurs in the opinion of El Cerrito Police Chief Forrest H. Wright that no mere grass fire would have caused such complete deterioration of the remains, or could account for the large crack in the skull.[19]

The Coroner's Jury concluded their investigation as a "hung jury" on December 28, 1927. Sadly for accurate history, they agreed with the version offered by that "Edison of Crime Detection," the Berkeley criminologist E.O. Heinrich. Despite the compelling evidence provided by Deputy Coroner Reifschneider and Police Chief Wright, the jury went with Heinrich's bizarre conclusions. These conclusions included Heinrich's claim that the skeletal remains were found lying on the ground, apparently unburied—rather than the accurate report of the charred skeleton being buried in swampy marshland. E.O. Heinrich's other conclusions were all equally absurd, leaving one to wonder if he had actually viewed the remains himself, or just rushed through his findings so that he could pursue cases that he found more interesting. This report of the findings, from the *San Francisco Chronicle*, illustrates just how shameful the conclusions of Heinrich and the coroner's jury were. The italics are by the authors of this book.

> El Cerrito's Mystery of Charred Bones
> Goes Unsolved
>
> Contra Costa Coroner's Jury Finds Death
> 'Due to Unknown Cause'
>
> Berkeley Criminologist Believes Victim
> Died While on Hike
>
> The El Cerrito hills *supposed murder mystery*, started in November with the findings of charred human bones *on a hillside*, was yesterday [December 28, 1927] placed in the files of unsolved cases when a Coroner's Jury was unable to fix responsibility or cause, and returned a verdict of death due to unknown cause.
>
> *The man whose bones were found on the hillside died of natural causes*, was the theory advanced by E.O. Heinrich, Berkeley criminologist, who investigated the case. Instead of being murdered and his body burned with chemicals, as at first supposed, Heinrich stated his theory at the inquest that *the man had taken seriously ill and dropped dead while hiking* in the El Cerrito hills.
>
> The body oils and fats seeping into the ground as the body decomposed *were mistaken for chemicals, he surmised.* In burning off the hills during the summer the body was evidently incinerated he explained. *That death occurred in early spring was supposed by Heinrich*, who based his statement upon the finding of young grass such as grows on hillsides at springtime.

> The case, at first taken as a murder mystery, came to light with the finding of charred human bones at an isolated point on the El Cerrito hillside, November 1 [*sic*: October 31] by Henry Marco. It was then thought that the man had been murdered and the body burned with chemicals. Coroner Aubrey Wilson of Contra Costa County conducted the inquest in Richmond.[20]

The Coroner's Jury findings of December 28, 1927, were "placed in the files of unsolved cases," and remained a cold case until the publication of this book. No record has been found concerning the final disposition of Leslie's remains, or where they were buried. Considering those remains consisted only of badly burned bones, it is possible those remaining bones were simply cremated, and disposed of.

We still don't have the exact date of Leslie's death—and probably never will. We can narrow it down to the period from the October 5, 1927, date on the *Seattle Times*, found buried with his skeleton, until October 31, 1927, when his burned skeleton was found, placed in the grave on top of that newspaper. That copy of the *Seattle Times* offers additional reasons for concluding that the skeletal remains belonged to Leslie. John Ralph Dean, Leslie's friend of forty years, was then living in Seattle. Leslie himself had lived in the state of Washington between 1914 and May 20, 1916, when he was interviewed by a *Seattle Times* reporter, as he left Washington for the last time.[21]

While it would appear that Leslie was murdered, we don't know the motive, nor the identity of the person (or persons) who may have killed him. Even if the mystery of exactly what happened at El Cerrito, California, during October 1927 could be resolved, it would hardly close the book on Buckskin Frank Leslie. Beyond his claim that he was "born near San Antonio, Texas," on March 18, 1842, until he arrived in San Francisco during July 1869, aboard the steamship *Portland*, nothing is known of Leslie's early life that has been verified.

Did he study medicine in Heidelberg, Germany? Did he return home to serve the Confederacy as either a cavalryman or as a bugler? Did he actually go to places such as Australia and the Fiji Islands? Was he a "college graduate," as John Ralph Dean would assert on several occasions? So far, none of these claims can be confirmed or denied. Some claims, such as Leslie being a deputy under Hickok, or as a scout under Custer, would appear to be made from whole cloth, but until Leslie's actual whereabouts can be documented, for most of the 1870s, they can't be dismissed entirely.

Future historians may succeed in closing some of the many gaps that still remain in the chronology of Leslie's life. What these future historians uncover will most likely include new exploits, real and imagined, along with new locations and people, many of them undoubtedly women, that were all part of the many lives of Nashville Franklyn "Buckskin Frank" Leslie.

Epilogue

During 1927, the same year that Leslie was murdered, Walter Noble Burns's book, *Tombstone: An Iliad of the Southwest*, was published. Leslie was mentioned in that book, but he was clearly a featured player. Earp was the star—and would remain so in the many books and articles, by other writers, that would follow. Soon after Leslie's 1927 murder, several people whom Leslie had known in Tombstone also began to pass from the scene:

Wyatt Earp died in Los Angeles, from cancer, on January 13, 1929. His 1931 biography by Stuart N. Lake would be the first of many books about Earp, supplemented with a never-ending stream of magazine articles. Hollywood movies, with major stars portraying Earp, and a 226-episode TV series starring Hugh O'Brian, ensured Earp "household word" status.

Louisa Emma (Bilicke) Babcock died in San Francisco on January 3, 1930, at the age of sixty-two. She had been twice-widowed, and was survived by her two sons. As a child in Tombstone, nearly fifty years earlier, Louisa and Buckskin Frank were the witnesses at the wedding between Mike Killeen and Mary Jane "May" Evans on April 13, 1880. Eighty-four days later, Louisa again served as a witness for the widowed Mary Jane "May" Killeen at her July 6, 1880, wedding to Buckskin Frank Leslie.

William Milton Breakenridge, who rode in Tombstone posses with Leslie, died in Tucson on January 31, 1931. He was eighty-four. Breakenridge had written his own 1928 memoir of his Tombstone years entitled *Helldorado: Bringing Law to the Mesquite*, in which he told of his experiences with Leslie.

John Philip Clum, the first mayor of Tombstone and founder of the *Tombstone Epitaph*, died in Los Angeles at the age of eighty on May 2,

1932. Clum, along with movie cowboys William S. Hart and Tom Mix, was a pallbearer at Wyatt Earp's funeral.

Elnora Torbert Cast Leslie, Buckskin Frank's last (known) wife died in Omak, Washington, on August 19, 1932, following a long illness. She was sixty-three-years-old at the time of her death, and had been living in Omak with her son, Burton A. Cast (1893-1963). She was survived by four other children as well as a brother and sister. Her funeral services were held in nearby Okanogan, Washington. Her obituary listed her children and siblings as survivors but made absolutely no mention of Buckskin Frank Leslie.

George Whitwell Parsons died in Los Angeles on January 5, 1933, at the age of eighty-two. His journals recording his time in the "Town Too Tough to Die" have left us a priceless look at that historic time and place. He was planning a trip with Leslie, and others, on the day that Leslie killed Billy Claiborne. Parsons also served as a pallbearer for Wyatt Earp, along with William S. Hart, Tom Mix and John P. Clum.

Colonel John Ralph Dean died in Seattle on July 31, 1936, at the age of seventy-two. The following day, the *Seattle Times* published an obituary that described Dean as a "veteran of three wars, one time captain of the Texas Rangers, pony express rider and frontier scout," which was over the top even by Dean standards. The widowed Dean was survived by his son and a granddaughter.

Mary Jane "May" Evans Killeen Leslie Durward was the last of Leslie's known wives to pass away. She was ninety at the time of her death on March 24, 1947—just six days after what would have been Leslie's 105th birthday. She had been a resident of Banning, California, for fifty-three years at the time of her death. She outlived three husbands. Only her last husband, Alexander Durward, died from natural causes.

Appendix A

[From the *Tombstone Weekly Epitaph,* November 18, 1882]

Leslie's Luck

"Billy the Kid" Takes a Shot at "Buckskin Frank."

The Latter Promptly Replies, and the Former Quietly Turns His Toes Up to the Daisies.

Tuesday morning about 7 o'clock another tragedy was added to the already long list that have dotted with crimson the history of our city. The causes which led to the affray, as far as known, are fully detailed in the testimony elicited at the coroner's inquest. The survivor of the sad affair, Frank Leslie, or "Buckskin Frank," is well known throughout the country. William Claiborne, alias the "Kid," who precipitated the affray which led to his sudden and untimely taking off, has in the past gained considerable notoriety by his connection with desperate characters and participation in deeds of violence. He was arrested something over a year ago for the murder of Hicks [*sic,* James Hickey], at Charleston, but upon being tried was acquitted. Whatever may have been his record in the past, there is no doubt that at the time he met his death he was engaged in an attempt at assassination, which was frustrated by the coolness and determination of his intended victim. Below we give the statement of Mr. Leslie concerning the unfortunate affair, which is fully corroborated by the testimony and verdict of the coroner's jury.

STATEMENT OF FRANK LESLIE.

I was talking with some friends in the Oriental saloon when Claiborne came in and pushed his way among us and began using very insulting language. I took him to one side and said, "Billy don't interfere, those people are friends among themselves, and are not talking about politics at all, and don't want you about." He appeared quite put out and used rather bad and certainly very nasty language towards me. I told him there was no use of him fighting with me, that there was no occasion for it, and leaving him joined my friends. He came back again and began using exceedingly abusive language, when I again took him by the collar of his coat and led him away, telling him not to get mad, that it was for his own good, that if he acted in that manner he was liable to get in trouble. He pushed away from me, using very harsh language, and as he started away shook his finger at me and said, "That's all right, Leslie, I'll get even with you," and went out of the saloon. In a short time a man came in and said there was a man waiting outside to shoot me, but I didn't pay much attention to it. A few minutes later another man came in looking quite white and said Claiborne was waiting outside with a rifle

TO SHOOT FRANK LESLIE

I then went out, and as I stepped on the sidewalk saw about a foot of a rifle barrel protruding from the end of the fruit stand. I stepped out in the street and saw it was Claiborne, and said "Billy, don't shoot, I don't want you to kill me, nor do I want to have to shoot you." Almost before I finished he raised the gun and shot, and I returned the fire from my pistol, aiming at his breast. As soon as I shot I saw him double up and had my pistol cocked and aimed at him again when I saw, or thought I saw, another man by him, putting his hands around him, and I lowered the pistol, and when it was discharged the bullet went in the sidewalk. After I fired, I advanced upon him, but not to shoot, when he said, "Don't shoot again; I am killed," which I didn't but watched him with my pistol at full cock, as I didn't know what game he might play to get me off my guard. At that moment officer Coyle came up and took hold of my pistol hand. I told him to be careful, as it was at full cock. I then uncocked it and gave it to him, and I said I would go with him. I told him that I was sorry; that I might have done more, but I couldn't do less. He then placed me under arrest.

Coroner Matthews impaneled a jury, which met at 1 o'clock p.m. at Ritter's undertaking rooms, and the following testimony concerning the killing was elicited:

W.J. MASON,

being duly sworn says: I reside in Tombstone. I recognize the body submitted to the jury as that of William Claiborne; have known him for three years. This morning I came to the Oriental saloon. While I was drinking alone, Mr. Claiborne came into the saloon and had some words with Mr. Leslie, and Claiborne said "I will see you later." Mr. Leslie replied, "While I am in Tombstone you can see me any time." Mr. Claiborne then left the saloon, and I left the saloon to see Mr. Brophy, and met Mr. Claiborne on the corner near the Oriental, Fifth and Allen. I advised him to wait and I would buy some fish and we would go to breakfast together. I advised him to do nothing but drop the matter and have no trouble. He said he did not propose to drop the matter, and would go and get his Winchester and would settle the matter at once. That is the last I seen of Mr. Claiborne in good health. I saw him next being behind the fruit stand beside the Oriental. He complained he was mortally wounded, saying "My backbone is all shot." I got on the ground in time [to] see Mr. Leslie hand his six-shooter to the officer, and being taken off by the officer. The next I saw of Mr. Claiborne was in the undertaker's office, dead. I did not see the shooting. I do not know of my own knowledge who killed Mr. Claiborne. Claiborne said that he had some trouble with some one and was going to get his Winchester and settle the matter, mentioning no names. He passed down Allen street with his gun in his hand towards the Oriental saloon. I was in Mr. Brophy's saloon when

I heard the shots. I did not know of any ill-feeling existing between the parties before this morning. I seen the officers take a rifle from the ground where Claiborne lay. I do not know the officer's name who took Leslie away. I only seen one rifle on the ground.

DR. G.C. WILLIS,

being first duly sworn, says: I reside in Tombstone; physician and surgeon by occupation. I saw Mr. Claiborne this morning a little before 8 o'clock at my office, being brought there by his friends in a condition of shock, bordering on collapse. I cut open his shirt and found a gun shot wound in the left side, and an opening in the back close to his spinal column, probably the wound of exit. He was not bleeding very much. He wanted to urinate, which he did. The urine contained blood. After that act his prostration was more complete I gave him stimulants. I dressed the wounds. Then he talked about his opponent and called him a murdering son of a b----. Having no convenience there, I sent him up to the hospital. There was no pulse at the wrist from the time he came in until he went out. The action of the heart was so feeble that I could hardly detect it. I did not probe the wound. In my opinion the ball must have passed through the spleen and through the left kidney in all probability, which would account for the blood in the urine, and probably injured the spinal column. In my opinion it was a fatal wound. He was not dead when he left the office. He spoke of giving a belt to Mr. Herring. I do not know which one of the Herrings it was. He was not wholly conscious. He said he [Leslie] was a murdering son of a b---- to shoot a man in the back. I was examining the back when he made that remark. I think he received the wound in front.

OTTO JOHNSON,

being duly sworn, says: I am a saloon keeper at Willcox. This morning as I was about to leave Judge Moses' saloon to go to breakfast at the Can Can chophouse, I saw Mr. Claiborne on the corner of Fifth and

Allen streets near Mr. Joyce's saloon, with a gun scabbard slung over his left shoulder and a Winchester in his right hand with his thumb on the trigger and the gun pointed downward. I said to him, "Hello, Bill, where are you going?" He came up to me and remarked, "I don't allow any man to spit on me, and if he wants a fight to come out here, and if he don't come out I will go in and make him fight." I asked him what he meant by that. He said, "A man by the name of Frank Leslie." I tried to talk him out of it and to take a walk down the street with me. He said no, if I interfered he would then turn loose on me. Thinking it better to take a walk, I walked into Joyce's saloon. I saw a friend of mine there by the name of Mr. Percy talking to two or three gentlemen there. I shook hands with Mr. Percy and asked him if he knew a man by the name of Frank Leslie. He said yes, and turned around to one of the gentlemen he was talking with, and introduced me to Frank Leslie. I told Mr. Leslie to be careful, that there was a man outside with a Winchester after him. Mr. Leslie asked me whereabouts. Told him outside the saloon. With that he walked to the side door on Fifth street, opened the door, stood there a minute and looked around. He closed the door and walked on the sidewalk. The next thing I heard was shots fired. I went outside, saw Mr. Claiborne lying on the sidewalk and Mr. Leslie about two feet from him with a gentleman holding up the hand that had his pistol in it. I walked away after that. I did not see the shots fired. Leslie left the saloon from the second side door of the saloon on Fifth street.

WILLIAM HENRY BUSH,

being duly sworn, says: I reside in Tombstone, occupation bootblack. Billy Claiborne came up the street with the gun on his shoulder and said, "I am going to kill Frank Leslie," He came to me and I said, "Billy, don't go over there, give me your gun." He said, "No, you black son of a b----, I will kill you." I got up by the door and saw Billy across the street, with his gun, and I hollered to the barkeeper in the Palace saloon that there was going to be a shooting scrape. I saw him raise the gun to shoot Mr. Leslie, and I seen the gun go off, the bullet striking the sidewalk. I heard two shots fired. I seen Mr. Leslie near the sidewalk near the Oriental, with the pistol in his hand. I did not know which was shooting. Claiborne fired first.

JOHN J. REILLY,

being duly sworn, says: I reside in Tombstone; occupation laborer. My attention was directed to Claiborne with a carbine or rifle in his hand. His remaining so long in one position on the sidewalk of the Oriental saloon close to the fruit stand caused me to watch him. He remained possibly ten minutes in the same position, gun pointed downward. When a man emerged from the middle door of the Oriental saloon on Fifth Street, Claiborne raised his rifle to his shoulder and fired. The attacked party at once stepped off the sidewalk back to me and began firing. I was standing at the corner of the Crystal Palace saloon. Being in range of the rifle I retreated behind the corner; heard other shots, but saw neither party fire them. As soon as the man emerged from the door the rifle was discharged. I am acquainted with both parties, Claiborne and Leslie, but did not recognize Leslie. I am positive there were three shots fired, and I think there were four. I am positive Claiborne fired the first shot. The second shot was fired almost instantly by the attacked party.

JAMES COYLE,

being duly sworn, says: I reside in Tombstone; am a policeman. About half past seven o'clock this morning I was standing opposite Cohn's cigar store on Allen street, talking to Dave Cohn. My back was toward the Oriental saloon. I heard a shot fired, and turned. I saw Leslie close to the sidewalk with a pistol in his hand. He fired, and I ran towards him. Before I got to him he fired again. He was standing on the sidewalk when I came up to him. He said "Jim, here is my pistol; be careful it is cocked." He laid the hammer down and gave it to me. He said, "I will go with you." He said, "Jimmy, I could have done more, but could not have done less. I did not want to kill him. He was laying to kill me." I picked up the rifle that was lying on Claiborne's knees, across his thighs. I took Leslie as far as the police court-room. I turned him over to Deputy Sheriff Cory there. I gave Cory the pistol and rifle. Claiborne was lying on the sidewalk, close to the fruit stand. I did not see Claiborne until I walked over, and did not know what Leslie was shooting at. I do not know who fired the first shot. There were two of the chambers of Leslie's pistol discharged. I heard three shots fired.

DAVID COHN,

being duly sworn, says: I reside in Tombstone; occupation, merchant. I saw Claiborne raise his rifle and fire the first shot; saw Leslie fire two shots afterwards. Claiborne was back of the end of fruit stand, near the door of the Oriental saloon. Leslie was standing facing him, about five or six feet from him. He was on the sidewalk. I did not see Leslie until the shooting commenced. I had seen Claiborne about ten minutes before the shooting. I am positive Claiborne fired the first shot. I saw Claiborne fall at the first shot fired by Leslie.

LEON JACOBS,

being duly sworn, says: I reside in Tombstone; occupation merchant. I have heard the statement of Mr. Cohn, and corroborate his statement.

E.H. DEAN,

being duly sworn, says: I reside in Tombstone; occupation, barkeeper at the Oriental saloon. Mr. Leslie came into the Oriental about one hour previous to the shooting. He and three others were standing at the end of the counter talking, when Mr. Claiborne came in. Mr. Claiborne stepped up to them and interfered in their conversation. He made a remark about Dave Neagle, and said that anyone that would vote for Ward was a son of a b-----. Mr. Leslie told him to go away from them, as they were not talking politics. He said he would not go away. Mr. Leslie took hold of him and pulled him away and told him he was liable to get into trouble with the other parties. He said that he wouldn't stay away. Leslie took hold of him the second time and threw him towards the opening into the other room. Claiborne told him he would allow no man to handle him in a manner of that kind. Mr. Leslie told him it was for his own good that he was pulling him away. Claiborne then left the house. The next I heard was a man came running in telling Mr. Leslie that Claiborne was outside with a rifle to kill him. Mr. Leslie then went out the side door on Fifth street. I went out of the side door, the first one above that. Mr. Leslie jumped off the sidewalk, about ten feet in middle of the street. There was a shot fired from where Mr. Claiborne was standing. Mr. Leslie then fired two shots. I did not see Mr. Claiborne before the shots were fired. He was standing at the end of the fruit stand, near the third door. I did not hear any threats made before he left the saloon, either by him or Leslie. Both parties had been drinking some. Leslie did not appear to be angry with Claiborne, but told him he was doing it for his own good. Claiborne was very angry when he left the saloon. Nothing was said about meeting later, by the parties, that I heard. It was about fifteen minutes after Claiborne left the saloon that Leslie was warned. I was on the sidewalk when the first shot was fired. Did not see who fired it. It was not Leslie who fired it.

THE CORONER'S VERDICT.

The testimony being concluded, the jury, after a few moments' deliberation returned the following verdict:

We, the undersigned, a jury of inquest, summoned and impaneled by the coroner of said county to inquire whose the body submitted to our inspection, when, where and under what circumstances he came to his death. After viewing the body and hearing such testimony as has been brought before us, find that his name was William Claiborne, age and nativity unknown, and that he came to his death from the effects of a pistol wound inflicted by Frank Leslie, in the town of Tombstone, Arizona

Territory, on the 14th day of November, 1882; and that the shooting was done in self-defense, and, in the opinion of the jury, was justifiable.

I.M. ISAACS	J.F. DURKEE
THOMAS M. YOUNG	DANIEL McCANN
PAT. HOLLAND	CHARLES LITTCHILD
GEORGE WILLIAMS	I. HART

Appendix B

From the *San Francisco Chronicle*, Saturday, December 2, 1893

IN THE YUMA PRISON.

The Fate of a Some-Time San Franciscan.
Frank Leslie Serving for
Life.

An Interesting Story—Whereabouts
Unknown to Most of His
Friends Here.

Occasionally there is a casual inquiry among old-timers for "Frank" Leslie, who used to keep a saloon on Hardie place, San Francisco, with the late James P. Kerr as his partner. The answer generally is "Oh, Leslie's down in Arizona somewhere, running a stock ranch or something."

In reality, N.F. Leslie, better known as "Frank," is serving a life sentence for murder in the Territorial Prison at Yuma, A.T.

He is a good-looking man of medium height, with regular features, aquiline nose, soft blue eyes and chestnut-brown hair tinged with gray. He is an interesting talker, a close student, well posted on the topics of the day, and his English is almost perfect.

The story of his life is a romance. Born in Virginia in 1842 of a good family he went to Heidelberg to study medicine, his brother at the same time going to West Point for a military education. When the Civil War broke out in 1861 Frank returned to his old home in Virginia and entered the Confederate army as a bugler, while his brother joined the Union forces. After the war Frank came West and at one time was a partner of the late James P. Kerr in a saloon on Hardie place in this city.

Tiring of city life, Leslie emigrated to Arizona, where for a number of years he served as a border scout, most of the time being chief of scouts. He was a favorite of the late General Crook, and has many a thrilling tale to tell of service under him during the early days of Arizona.

About six years ago, in partnership with the late Milton E. Joyce of the Café Royal, San Francisco, Leslie bought a large stock ranch nineteen miles from Tombstone and about twenty miles from the Mexican border, and went extensively into the cattle business. Life on the ranch soon became lonesome and monotonous, so he brought a young girl from Oakland to his home. They became very much attached to each other, and a year and a half after her arrival he proposed marriage to her and she accepted. Everything looked bright for Leslie. Business was thriving and he was a thoroughly happy man.

They were to be married in Tombstone, but the girl kept putting it off. Finally a day was set and together they rode on horseback into Tombstone early one morning. They were to be married at noon, but she kept putting off the hour. Leslie could not understand it, but believed her conduct to be only a nervous woman's whim.

Finally, at 9 o'clock in the evening, as they were going to the justice's house, she told him she was a married woman—had been married for four years. Her husband, she said was then living in Tucson. She had left him, but was never divorced.

They rode back that night to the ranch. Leslie said nothing to the girl, brooding in silence over his great trouble. One evening on his return from Tombstone he found the girl on the porch of the ranch house. She and the foreman of the ranch had been drinking during his absence and there was no doubt of their relationship. He upbraided her and harsh words followed. His story is that she drew his pistol, which she had secreted on her person. As she pulled the trigger he threw up his arm and sent the weapon flying. Furious with rage he reached into his room through an open window and got a small revolver which belonged to the girl and fired two shots.

When the shooting commenced, the foreman stepped into the house for his rifle, and as he showed his face outside the door Leslie put a bullet into him. The wounded man fell off the porch and made his way to a neighbor's house, where, after a long illness, he finally recovered. After the girl was shot she crawled around to the back of the house and died. Leslie put up his horse and returned to the porch, where he lay all night in sort of a stupor. In the morning he went to the back of the house and found the girl dead. He immediately rode into Tombstone and gave himself up. When the trial came up his lawyers were in another part of the Territory. They advised him to make no defense as he could not be convicted on the evidence. This he did, pleading not guilty. He was convicted and sentenced to life imprisonment.

This is Leslie's story. Whether true or not it is a sad one. He is the prison druggist and has many privileges. He does not wear the prison garb and is not confined to a cell at night. His conduct is perfect. Superintendent Gates said he was the best-behaved prisoner, as well as the most useful, in the penitentiary. In case of sickness the physician is called in and diagnoses the case, while Leslie fills the prescription and administers the medicine. His drug store is the acme of neatness.

Leslie is 51 years old now, but does not look over 40. He has been in prison three and a half years and has strong hopes of being pardoned in a few years.

W. H. CAMERON.

Appendix C

From the *San Francisco Call*, Sunday, January 7, 1900

Personal Experiences With the Late General Lawton

Told by Capt. N. Frank Leslie, His Chief of Scouts in the Apache Campaign.

A Story by the Man Whom Lawton Had Asked to Take a Position on His Staff in the Philippine Islands.

My work with General Lawton commenced with a chase after one Geronimo, and was ended by another Geronimo of another race, on the opposite side of the earth. I knew Lawton when he was a private, fighting his way through more than thirty battles of the Civil War, from the ranks to a commission.

I was his chief of scouts when we walked and climbed 800 miles through the Sierra Madre. I was with him in Cuba, and had been asked and was preparing to take a place on his staff in the Philippine when he was killed in his engagement with General [Licerio] Geronimo.

People here may feel sorry for Lawton's death, but you cannot feel it as we do in Arizona. We knew the man there. Not the general; just the man who could trail an Indian into his own country and then outwalk him, outwit him in his own stratagem, undergo the same privations, and finally herd and drive that wild Indian into a trap, broken in spirit and strength. Even then the Indians respected him for his wonderful personal courage, and would surrender to no other person.

The fight with Geronimo, the Apache, was when Lawton was a captain in the Fourth Cavalry. Geronimo had about 150 Apaches with him. In the force sent across the border to take him there were less than fifty soldiers and something more than twice that number of Chiricahua Indian scouts. The Apaches had left the reservation well supplied with arms and ammunition, and had put in their time driving stock across the line until that part of the Sierra Madre where they were lodged was a regular stock range, with plenty of ponies to ride and cattle for food.

The Indians were well fixed for a long fight. They had no fear of the Mexicans, either civilians or soldiers. They were safe from attack from the Americans by reason of being out of our territory. They had transportation and food wherever they might be, for the cattle and ponies wandered at will over a large range, and the Indians knew the sheltered and grassy valleys where they could be found.

The policy was not to attack them in any one pitched battle, but to take them as a hunter and his dog would hunt quail.

They were rapidly driven ahead of us. My Chiricahua scouts kept us always informed as to where they were, and we moved after rapidly enough to keep them always alarmed and on the go.

A sudden attack and pitched battle might have enabled us to kill some and scatter the rest, but it would have been impossible for us to follow or find them if separated. The Indians had heretofore been safe when they retreated to the Mexican side of the line, but now a special treaty had been arranged, permitting us to follow them wherever they went, crossing and re-crossing the line at our pleasure something which was very necessary, as to going up and down what is called "Give and Take" Canyon the crooked valley many times crosses the boundary line, which is straight at that point.

The Mexican soldiers were hardly worth being called soldiers, they were not paid, fed nor drilled with any regularity. No scouts or transportation were provided for them, and when they went out to repel invading bands of Apaches they seldom escaped without painful experience.

The Apaches were careful to save ammunition whenever possible and one of their economies was to lie in wait at the head of a barranca [steep-walled ravine or gorge] or on the walls of one of the many cienegas [a spring in a marshy area at the foot of a mountain] through which the Mexicans must pass. When the scoutless Mexicans came walking, beneath the trap, the Indians would industriously tumble rocks over upon them, sometimes killing and wounding soldiers, stampeding their pack trains and demoralizing them completely.

We started out with a well equipped pack train, but as we got farther up into the high Sierra we gradually lost or were compelled to leave our pack animals. Many of them fell over the edges of the trail and were killed by the fall, others were so injured that they had to be shot. As we entered this rough country we found that the Indians were also losing ponies and many of them were still alive but exhausted and dying. Some had been killed and partly cut up and eaten, for an Indian, especially an Apache, is always fond of horse meat and they seem to eat it indifferently, even when they could obtain beef. They always carried a supply of it cut into long strings so that it might dry as they traveled. As our chase became more serious the enemy took to still higher land. We discarded all of our packing outfit and each man, officer, soldier or scout came to the same level, each carried his own provisions, gun and single blanket to protect from the cold, which was very bitter in the high altitude and thin light air, for up hill or down we were always at an elevation of over five thousand feet or more. The entire mountains seemed to be nothing but grotesque heaps of volcanic lava, deep canyons with sides too precipitous to be traveled, and between them mesas covered with flowering cactus and mesquite.

The whole place was as lonesome as the moon and I do not know of any place on earth that more resembles it. Cold, bleak and with an inexpressible lonesomeness that filled the mind with forebodings.

As Geronimo, Natchez and the rest of the band became harder pressed they took to higher and more inaccessible peaks and always made their camps on the highest land in reach. Here they were made uncomfortable and filled with a dread of something that they could not understand. The flashes from our heliograph signalers were almost always in view, as messages were being sent back and forth over the peaks. This was something that they could not understand and was attributed by them to spirit agency. They would never attempt to scale any of the peaks from which they had seen these flashes and their territory became more and more limited. The men would never work. Their hands showed that such had been their habit for generations, for wrists were actually larger than the hand, as we found afterward when we tried to handcuff them.

The women, overcome and exhausted by the superhuman tasks of attempting to provide fuel and water for the camps of the mountain peaks, were unable to nurse or feed their starving children and rather than leave them to be eaten by coyotes or panthers threw them to their deaths in the gloomy canyons.

The squaws were dressed in trousers, with shirts worn loose as blouses over them, and rode straddle, so we had no way of distinguishing them from the men and often found that we had killed by mistake a mother or a young girl when shooting at what appeared to be one of the warriors.

Toward the last the Indians had lost all of their horses, we too were on foot, our supply trains far below, and the whole chase was nothing but a succession of climbs up one cliff and down another.

My scouts never once made a mistake as to the position of Geronimo, and while he was ever planning ambushes for us we usually turned the tables on him by getting around on the point behind him and so driving him hurriedly down the very cliff over which he had intended to roll rocks down upon us, as he had usually been able to do with the Mexicans.

These latter now became bolder as they found that we had about conquered the Apaches, and on one occasion became insolent and fired upon our Chiricahua scouts, pretending that they did not know that we were in their territory by authority.

The final surrender of Geronimo took place in what was known as Skeleton Canyon, a deep gorge eleven miles from the Mexican boundary.

It took its name from a massacre which occurred there long before, when the guards and mules of a pack train loaded with Mexican dollars were killed by bandits. In the mix-up many of the rawhide sacks of dollars were burst open and scattered about, and even to the present time it is still possible to find those melancholy souvenirs scattered here and there about the desolate rocks.

At last the time came when Geronimo sent a squaw into camp to say that he wanted to see Lawton, who was then rounding up the last of the scattered outsiders. Lieutenant [Charles B.] Gatewood took a few men and went to see Geronimo, but returned discouraged and said that he thought that the Indians were only attempting to gain time and that any communication was dangerous. It was impossible from their location and from the wornout condition of our troops to attempt to kill or capture them by force.

Our scouts, the main body of our force, were themselves Chiricahuas, blood relatives to those whom we were fighting. They had slept in the same wigwams, hunted and raided together. To attempt to get our men to kill their chums and kin would surely have resulted in their murdering us all, joining forces with the outlaws, and then with a new supply of ammunition from our stores they would have started another series of raids and massacres with the certainty of a clear field of action for some time, as it could not have then been possible to get another band of scouts to work under American control, and without them there could be no success.

Lawton said that Geronimo had not made his offer in bad faith and went out the next morning to meet him. He succeeded in obtaining a promise of surrender.

Geronimo and the remnants of his band slunk into Skeleton Canyon, broken-spirited and ashamed. Their children were gone, some of their wives were dead and some lost. Indians are not demonstrative, but their feelings are none the less keen because concealed.

These Apaches felt themselves but women before their captors. Lawton himself was gaunt, ragged and lean, having lost forty pounds in weight, but his face was sparkling with joy at the successful end of as hard a fight as ever Hannibal saw. Not killed by sudden advantage, but outrivaled, outgeneraled, and beaten in a fair test of endurance. The chase had covered over a thousand miles of travel and had been a life and death struggle for every in it, the hunters as well as the game.

The early part of the day was spent in gathering in the Indians, telling them what was expected of them and preparing for an early start next day. As the afternoon wore away the intense heat was followed by threatening clouds, shutting in the canyon, and then came a tempest with continuous explosions of electricity with which the air was charged and a smashing rain that drove us all—officers, soldiers, scouts and prisoners—into covered wagons for shelter.

A wild, dramatic ending to the play, with murderers in the skeleton-covered canyon, that was itself a stage where murders had been. This was the fourth surrender of Geronimo and the last.

There were a few straggling Indians that could not be found or induced to come in who were miserably killed by the Mexican soldiers, now brave when danger was over, and the backbone of the enemy broken.

The Indians were finally started East in charge of Lawton to leave forever the land of their fathers; some to go to Carlisle. [Carlisle Indian Industrial School in Pennsylvania] and some to Florida.

Even at that time, when Lawton was only a captain of cavalry, General [Nelson A.] Miles held him in the highest esteem and said of him: "I selected from Fort Huachuca an officer by the name of Captain H.W. Lawton of the Fourth United States Cavalry, whom I thought would fulfill all of the requirements of commander for the reason that he believed that these Indians could be subjugated." Lawton, although he recognized their great skill, cunning and physical strength, believed that they could be met and defeated by studying and improving their own methods. He was peculiarly fitted for carrying out this idea. Physically he was in perfect condition, weighing two hundred and thirty pounds, well proportioned, straight, agile, full of energy and without superfluous flesh. He could take up an ordinary man and throw him a rod. He had a bright, handsome face and was in the prime of life. As fine a specimen of man as could be found.

When [Theodore] Roosevelt commenced his recruitment I enlisted in one of the first companies formed in Arizona, and after arriving in Cuba was transferred by my own request to Lawton's command and remained with him until the end of Spain's domination in the Western hemisphere.

At the end of the war I returned to Arizona. A short time ago I received a request from General Lawton to join him in the Philippines and take a position on his staff, as he wished to scout and wear out the guerrilla bands there in the same way that the Apaches had been subdued.

His death leaves me thinking of things of which I would not care to speak. I can only think of the two Geronimos, one the last of his race to submit, the other the last leader of organized troops in the Philippines, and the life of Lawton between.

Notes

Endnotes to Chapter One

1. Register of Custom Employees at Small Ports, Vol. 4, No. 6, March 13, 1886, letter from the Collector of Customs, El Paso, Texas to Secretary of the Treasury, enclosing Nashville Franklyn Leslie's application for employment dated March 10, 1886, National Archives and Records Administration, Washington, D.C. It is significant that Leslie spelled his middle name "Franklyn" (as opposed to "Franklin") on this as well as other documents that bear his full signature. While it may appear to be a minor point, there is the possibility that "Franklyn" could have been a surname from his family tree that may aid in resolving his antecedents.

2. *Arizona Weekly Citizen* (Tucson) Sunday, March 27, 1881.

3. *Tombstone Daily Prospector*, Monday, July 15, 1889. This article also asserted that "his father's name was Kennedy," and that his "mother's maiden name was Leslie." So far, no solid documentation has been located in Galveston that would support this claim by the *Tombstone Daily Prospector.* The closest candidate was a person identified only as "Kennedy" who appears on the *Galveston County Tax Rolls* for 1852 and 1860.

4. *1886 Great Register for Cochise County A[rizona] T[erritory]* information courtesy William "Billy" Mills.

5. *Texas Wills and Probate Minutes, 1833 to 1974.* Vol. J-K, 1883-1884. Bexar County Court.

6. *Bexar County Tax Rolls* —Tax Assessments.

7. *San Francisco Chronicle*, Saturday, December 2, 1893. This quotation is from a profile of Leslie written by a reporter named W.H. Cameron.

ENDNOTES TO CHAPTER TWO

1. *Daily Alta California* (San Francisco), Sunday, July 11, 1869. This newspaper's list of the arriving passengers on the steamship *Portland* used only commas for punctuation and omitted periods. It read as follows: "Portland—Per Pacific—Capt Roxby, Capt Fletcher, F Reischer, Miss O Mercier, G Gregg and wife, A P Miller, William Derrick, J Olson, G McCauley, Solomon Strong, C W Claus, F W King, I Patterson, J R Lake, J Buston, H Wolff, J Hartley, T J Cottle, M R Landon, Charles Hodge and wife, J S Walker, and wife, Miss McIntier, Henry Rhoades, Miss L Landers, Miss E Lycon, H W Rapplye, N F Leslie, J J Harris, J W Felt, Fred Wilson, F F Dickinson, B L Stone, C Finlay and son, J Rainbow, J G Jeffers and son, R Landers, Mrs M Hochguth, Colonel West (Wells, Fargo & Co's messenger) and 26 others."

2. Tom Horn, *Life of Tom Horn* (1904), 42.

3. Lorenzo D. Walters, *Tombstone's Yesterday* (1928), 23.

4. Larry D. Ball, *Tom Horn: In Life and Legend* (2014), 45.

5. Don Chaput, *"Buckskin Frank" Leslie* (1999), 123n5.

6. *San Francisco City Directory*, 1878, 515.

7. Ibid., 1879, 527. The owners of Kerr & Jurado's Saloon & Billiard Room died just over a year apart. James P. Kerr was in Denver when he became ill and died according to an obituary published in the *San Francisco Chronicle* on July 8, 1892. Thomas A. Jurado died in San Francisco on August 12,1893, at the age of 46, according to an obituary published in the *San Francisco Call* on August 14, 1893.

8. *San Francisco Chronicle*, Saturday, December 2, 1893.

9. *San Francisco City Directory*, 1880, 546.

10. William H. Knapp was born in New York State in 1852. He was the eldest of eight children born to Robert Israel Knapp (1833-1904) and

Elizabeth Minerva Misner. By the time the 1870 census was taken, Robert and Elizabeth Knapp, along with their six children, had moved across the continent and were living in Sonoma County, California, Sometime during the next decade, somewhere in California, William K. Knapp and Frank Leslie became friends.

11. *Bisbee Daily Review* (Arizona), Tuesday, March 27, 1934.

12. Philip J. Rasch, "A Note on Buckskin Frank Leslie" (1954), 9.

13. *Arizona Quarterly Illustrated*, July 1880, 11.

14. Carl Gustave Bilicke (1828-1896) was a native of Brandenberg, Germany. He and his son, Albert C. Bilicke (1561-1915), owned the Cosmopolitan Hotel from 1879 to 1882. After the Cosmopolitan burned down, they relocated in Los Angeles where they made a fortune. At the time of Albert's death he owned several four-star resorts and hotels, and had a net worth of $1,500,000 (in 1915 dollars). Albert Bilicke and his wife were among the victims who suffered on the *Lusitania* when it sank on May 7, 1915. Mrs. Bilicke survived but her husband did not.

15. 1880 U.S. Federal Census for Tombstone Village, Pima County, Arizona.

16. Mrs. "May" Killeen was born in Kentucky as Mary Jane Evans on May 25, 1856. Her first husband, Michael D. "Mike" Killeen was born in Illinois in 1848. He was listed as being a "Saloon keeper" in Tombstone on the 1880 U.S. Federal Census. On census records, the term "saloon keeper" did not always denote someone being the actual owner of a saloon. In Killeen's case he was employed as a bartender at Lowry and Archer's Saloon when the 1880 census was taken.

Endnotes to Chapter Three

1. The 1880 Pima County Census lists a "C.T. Packwood" who is probably this man who heard the deathbed statement of Killeen. He is

shown to be a forty-five-year-old miner, native of Pennsylvania, married but residing alone. Pima County, Arizona Census, enumerated June 7, 1880, 172.

2. *Tombstone Daily Epitaph*, Tuesday, August 24, 1880.

3. *Reno Gazette-Journal* (Nevada), Saturday, June 26, 1880.

4. *Powers of Attorney Book One*, 439-40. Found in Cochise County Recorder's Office, Bisbee, Arizona.

5. *Records of the Justice's Court of James Reilly*, Docket "A," 159. Precinct No. 17, Pima County, Arizona. Pima County was divided on February 1, 1881, and Tombstone became part of the new Cochise County. In the various biographies of Leslie the wedding date is usually given as August 5, 1880. The document signed by James Reilly clearly established that July 6, 1880, is the correct date for the nuptials.

6. Louisa Emma Bilicke was born on May 11, 1867, in Boise, Idaho. After her family left Tombstone, Louisa married Oramel McHenry (1861-1906) on March 3, 1886. They had four children, only two of whom lived to become adults. Louisa married her second husband, James H. Babcock (1874-1919) on August 8, 1910. She died at the age of 62 in San Francisco on January 3, 1930.

7. *Tombstone Daily Epitaph*, Thursday, July 22, 1880. James Vizina and Benjamin Cook were the actual owners of the building that became the Oriental Saloon. The building was leased to Milton E. Joyce and William C. Parker of San Francisco. Lou Rickabaugh, also of San Francisco, ran the gambling concession at the Oriental with William H. Harris and Richard Clark.

8. 1880 U.S. Federal Census for Tombstone Village, Pima County, Arizona.

9. *California Great Registers—Voter Registrations*, "October 18,1876 — Milton Edward Joyce, San Francisco."

10. George Whitwell Parsons, *The Private Journal of George W. Parsons* (1972), 69.

11. Leslie's testimony is given in Traywick, *Tombstone's Buckskin Frank: Nashville Franklyn Leslie* (2013), 25.

12. *Tombstone Daily Epitaph*, Wednesday, August 25, 1880.

13. *Arizona Weekly Citizen* (Tucson), Saturday, October 2, 1880.

14. *Arizona Daily Star* (Tucson), Saturday, October 30, 1880.

15. *Tombstone Daily Epitaph*, Thursday, September 23, 1880.

16. Cochise County Recorder's Office, Mill Sites, Book One, 110-11.

17. *Arizona Daily Star* (Tucson), Wednesday, September 29, 1880.

18. *Tombstone Daily Epitaph*, Wednesday, October 27, 1880.

19. *Arizona Daily Star* (Tucson), Saturday, October 30, 1880.

20. *Tombstone Nugget*, Friday, November 12, 1880.

21. *Minute Book*, Common Council, Village of Tombstone, 24. See also Alford E. Turner, *The Earps Talk* (1980), 24 and Gary L. Roberts, *Doc Holliday: The Life and the Legend* (2006), 131 and 446.

22. *Tombstone Daily Epitaph*, December 14, 1880.

Endnotes to Chapter Four

1. Leslie's original letter is part of the Colt Collection at the Connecticut State Library in Hartford.

2. *Arizona Weekly Citizen* (Tucson), March 27, 1881. This was a reprint of an item from a Tombstone newspaper of the previous week that is no longer available.

3. George W. Parsons's diary entry for March 22, 1881. Collection of the Arizona Historical Society.

4. William M. Breakenridge, *Helldorado: Bringing the Law to the Mesquite* (1928), 123.

5. *Tombstone Daily Epitaph*, Friday, April 15, 1881.

6. *Territory of Arizona v J.H. Holliday, April 15, 1881*, Docket Book, Recorder's Court, City of Tombstone.

7. *Official Oaths and Bonds*, Cochise County Recorder's Office.

8. Neil B. Carmony, *Tombstone's Violent Years, 1880-1882, As Remembered by John Plesent Gray*, 21-23.

9. *Tombstone Daily Nugget*, Monday, August 20, 1881.

10. *Tombstone Daily Epitaph*, Sunday, November 13, 1881.

11. Ibid.

12. Dempsey and Baldwin, *The Triumphs and Trials of Lotta Crabtree*, 261-70.

13. *Tombstone Daily Epitaph*, Thursday, December 8, 1881.

14. *The Weekly Arizona Miner* (Prescott), Friday, December 23, 1881, reprinting an item from the *Tombstone Tribune.*

15. *Tombstone Weekly Epitaph*, Monday, December 19, 1881.

Endnotes to Chapter Five

1. *Names of Mine Locations, Book III*: "Kansas King" 261, "Copper King" 262, and "Moira" 263. Found in Cochise County Recorder's Office.

2. *Deed of Mines, Book 5*, 384-86, Cochise County Recorder's Office.

3. *Tombstone Daily Epitaph*, Tuesday, January 10, 1882.

4. Ibid., Sunday, February 5, 1882.

5. Ibid., Thursday, March 16, 1882.

6. *Tombstone Nugget*, Thursday, March 16, 1882.

7. *Tombstone Daily Epitaph*, March 20, 1882.

8. *Tombstone Weekly Epitaph*, Monday, April 10, 1882.

9. *Tombstone Daily Epitaph*, Monday, May 1, 1882.

10. *Tombstone Daily Nugget*, Monday, May 1, 1882.

11. *Tombstone Daily Epitaph*, Monday, May 1, 1882.

12. William H. Knapp moved on to Tucson, where, on March 26, 1883, he married Jennie McMillan.

13. *Tombstone Daily Epitaph*, Wednesday, June 7, 1882. This was an 1882 census for Cochise County, Territory of Arizona, and not the 1880 U.S. Federal Census. In this census Leslie was listed as "Nashville Frank Leslie," a 40-year-old "saloon keeper" in Tombstone.

Endnotes to Chapter Six

1. *Tombstone Weekly Epitaph*, July 22, 1882.

2. Walter Noble Burns, *Tombstone: An Iliad of the Southwest* (1927), 266-67.

3. Lorenzo D. Walters, *Tombstone's Yesterday* (1928), 99.

4. William M. Breakenridge, *Helldorado: Bringing the Law to the Mesquite* (1928), 189.

5. Fred Dodge, *Under Cover for Wells Fargo: The Unvarnished Recollections of Fred Dodge* (1969), 240.

6. Charles Leland Sonnichsen, *Billy King's Tombstone* (1942) 31-32. This book contains an entire 23-page chapter entitled "Buckskin Frank Leslie: The Story of an Arizona Gunman." The excerpt here contains several errors, the most notable example having Ringo and Leslie meet "not long after Billy Claiborne was buried," when, in fact, Ringo died four months

before Leslie killed Claiborne. Unfortunately, that entire chapter devoted to Leslie is replete with similar inaccuracies.

7. *Deeds of Mines, Book 6*, 106-08, filed September 11, 1882, Cochise County Recorder's Office.

8. *Tombstone Weekly Epitaph*, Saturday, September 23, 1882.

9. Ibid., Saturday, October 7, 1882.

ENDNOTES TO CHAPTER SEVEN

1. *Tombstone Weekly Epitaph*, Saturday, October 28, 1882.

2. Ibid., Saturday, November 11, 1882.

3. Ibid., Saturday, November 18, 1882.

4. George W. Parsons's diary entry for November 14, 1882, Arizona Historical Society.

5. Lorenzo D. Walters, *Tombstone's Yesterday* (1928), 215.

6. *Tombstone Daily Epitaph*, Saturday, November 18, 1882.

ENDNOTES TO CHAPTER EIGHT

1. *Los Angeles Times*, Thursday, November 9, 1882.

2. *Arizona Weekly Citizen* (Tucson), Sunday, December 24, 1882.

3. *Arizona Daily Star* (Tucson), Sunday, February 18, 1883.

4. Ibid., Thursday, February 22, 1883.

5. Ibid., Tuesday, February 27, 1883.

6. *Sacramento Daily Record-Union*, Thursday, March 15, 1883.

7. *Truckee Tribune* (California), Saturday, March 13, 1869.

8. *Los Angeles Daily Herald*, Thursday, September 28, 1875.

9. Smith and Tingley, *The History of the Comstock Lode, 1850-1997*, 225.

10. *Los Angeles Daily Herald*, Wednesday, March 28, 1883.

11. *Arizona Daily Star* (Tucson), Tuesday, April 3, 1883.

12. Ibid., Thursday, April 19, 1883.

13. Bourke, *On the Border With Crook*, 456.

14. *Arizona Weekly Citizen* (Tucson) Saturday, April 21, 1883.

15. *Santa Fe Daily New Mexican*, Friday, April 20, 1883.

16. *Arizona Weekly Citizen* (Tucson), Saturday, May 5, 1883.

17. Ibid., Saturday, May 19, 1883.

18. *Arizona Daily Star* (Tucson), Sunday, June 3, 1883.

19. *Records of the Quartermaster General. Persons and Articles Hired at Ft. Huachuca, Arizona June 1883—In the Field.* Found in the National Archives and Records Administration, Washington, D.C.

20. *Marks and Brands*, 50-51, Cochise County Recorder's Office. This was not a precursor of the famous soft-drink of the same name. The soda was created in 1929 by Charles Leiper Grigg. The original lengthy name of "Bib-Label Lithiated Lemon-Lime Soda" was shortened to "7Up" in 1936. *Wikipedia: The Free Encyclopedia*, accessed January 16, 2017.

21. *Sacramento Daily Record-Union*, Tuesday, August 7, 1883.

22. *Arizona Weekly Citizen* (Tucson), Saturday, October 20, 1883.

23. *Weekly Phoenix Herald*, Thursday, November 8, 1883.

24. *Arizona Daily Star* (Tucson), Saturday, March 1, 1884.

25. *Great Register of the County of Cochise, Territory of Arizona, For the Year 1884.* Leslie's name appears on page 14 of the document. A

facsimile edition was published in 1984 by Tombstone Commemorative Enterprises, based in Tombstone, Arizona.

26. Indenture, December 26, 1884, *Deeds of Mines, Book 8*, 469-70, Cochise County Recorder's Office.

ENDNOTES TO CHAPTER NINE

1. *Records of the Quartermaster General.* "Persons and Articles Hired at Ft. Huachuca, Arizona, June 1885." Found in the National Archives and Records Administration, Washington, D.C.

2. *Arizona Weekly Citizen* (Tucson), Saturday, June 20, 1885.

3. "Roster of Troops Department of Arizona, Operating Against Hostile Chiricahuas, July 14, 1885, in the Sierra Madre," Southwest Museum, Los Angeles, California.

4. *Arizona Daily Star* (Tucson), Saturday, August 1, 1885.

5. *Santa Cruz Sentinel* (California), Sunday, July 12, 1885.

6. *Daily Tombstone*, Friday, July 31, 1885.

7. *Arizona Weekly Citizen* (Tucson), Saturday, August 29, 1885.

8. Crook's report as quoted in Dan L. Thrapp's *Al Sieber: Chief of Scouts*, 303-04.

9. *Arizona Daily Star* (Tucson),Tuesday, August 18, 1885.

10. National Archives to Philip J. Rasch, March 18, 1952, "Quartermaster General Settlement No. 8031 October 24, 1885," contained in the Philip J. Rasch Collection, Arizona Historical Society.

11. *Daily Tombstone*, Tuesday, October 27, 1885.

12. *Tombstone Daily Epitaph*, Thursday, January 14, 1886.

13. Ibid., Thursday, January 28, 1886.

14. Ibid., Sunday, February 14, 1886.

15. Ibid, Wednesday, March 10, 1886.

16. *Register of Customs Employees at Small Ports* 4, no. 6 (March 10, 1886): 338. Application for Employment from Nashville Franklyn Leslie to Collector of Customs Joseph Magoffin, National Archives and Records Administration, Washington, D.C.

17. *San Jose Evening News* (California), Thursday, March 11, 1886.

18. *Tombstone Daily Epitaph*, Friday, March 26, 1886.

19. Crook's entries from Odie B. Faulk's *The Geronimo Campaign* (1969), 92.

20. *Tombstone Daily Epitaph*, Sunday, April 4, 1886.

21. *San Francisco Chronicle*, Sunday, April 4, 1886.

22. *Los Angeles Times*, Saturday, April 17, 1886.

23. Charles Fletcher Lummis, *General Crook and the Apache Wars*, 21. Charles Fletcher Lummis was born on March 1, 1859, in Lynn, Massachusetts. He went to Harvard where he was a classmate of Theodore Roosevelt. He was a journalist and Indian rights activist. He was working for a Cincinnati newspaper when he received an offer to join the staff of the *Los Angeles Times*, which had been founded on December 4, 1881. Lummis accepted the offer and made the unusual decision to make the journey from Cincinnati to Los Angeles on foot, which took him 143 days. Upon his arrival he became the city editor of the *Los Angeles Times*. He remained in that position until 1888, when he suffered a mild stroke that left his left side paralyzed. The stroke hardly slowed him down, and he went on to have a colorful, event-filled, life. He died in Los Angeles on November 24, 1928.

24. *Tombstone Weekly Epitaph*, Sunday, April 25, 1886.

25. *Daily Tombstone*, Thursday, May 13, 1886.

26. Ibid., Tuesday, May 18, 1886.

27. Ibid., Monday, May 17, 1886.

28. Ibid., Tuesday, May 18, 1886.

29. Ibid.

30. *Tombstone Daily Epitaph*, Thursday, June 10, 1886.

31. *St. Johns Herald* (St. Johns, Arizona) Thursday, July 15, 1886, reprinting an item from an undated *Tombstone Democrat*.

32. *Register of Customs Employees at Small Ports* 4, no. 6 (July 13, 1886): 338. Letter of resignation from Nashville Franklyn Leslie to Collector of Customs Joseph Magoffin, National Archives and Records Administration, Washington, D.C.

33. *Tombstone Daily Epitaph*, Saturday, September 11, 1886.

NOTES TO CHAPTER TEN

1. *Marriage Book, Cochise County, Arizona*, Vol. 1, 109.

2. *Chicago Inter Ocean*, Sunday, November 25, 1892.

3. In the "St. Crispin's Day" speech in Shakespeare's *Henry V* (Act IV, iii, lines 49-51) the title character tells his assembled army: "Old men forget; yet all shall be forgot,/ But he'll remember, with advantages,/ What feats he did that day."

4. *Tombstone Daily Epitaph*, Tuesday, February 11, 1887.

5. Ibid., Wednesday, March 9, 1887.

6. *Tombstone Democrat*, Wednesday, March 9, 1887.

7. *Tombstone Daily Epitaph*, Tuesday, March 22, 1887.

8. *Santa Cruz Sentinel* (California), Tuesday, May 10, 1887.

9. No. 1218, *May Leslie vs. N. Frank Leslie,* Judgment and Decree, June 3, 1887, District Court, First Judicial District, Cochise County, Tombstone, Arizona.

10. Walter Noble Burns, *Tombstone: An Iliad of the Southwest* (1927) 161-63. As ridiculous as this account by Burns was, it would be repeated by generations of pulp writers —and historians, some of whom tried to spice up the "Silhouette Girl" story by having May Leslie pose for her pistol portraits in the nude.

11. *Tombstone Weekly Epitaph,* Sunday, June 12, 1887.

12. *Tombstone Daily Epitaph,* Thursday, June 16, 1887.

13. *Tombstone Weekly Epitaph,* Sunday, June 19, 1887.

14. Ibid., Sunday, July 17, 1887.

15. Ibid., Saturday, September 10, 1887.

16. *Tombstone Prospector,* Sunday, October 23, 1887.

17. *Tombstone Weekly Epitaph,* Saturday, February 4, 1887.

18. *Record of Mines, Book 11,* 621, Cochise County Recorder's Office.

19. *Tombstone Prospector,* Monday, January 21, 1889.

20. *Los Angeles Herald,* Tuesday, March 5, 1889.

21. *Tombstone Prospector,* Saturday, April 6, 1889.

22. *Sierra County Advocate* (Hillsborough, New Mexico) Tuesday, May 28, 1889.

23. Mollie Edwards was most likely her real name. Other contemporary accounts identified her as "Mollie Williams." She was also known as "Mollie Bradshaw," when she was living with a man named Bradshaw, who, according to unproven gossip, was killed when he had his head bashed in by Leslie.

24. *Tombstone Daily Epitaph,* Friday, July 12, 1889.

25. *Arizona Weekly Citizen* (Tucson), Saturday, July 20, 1889.

26. *Inquest Held on the Body of Mollie Edwards, July 14, 1889*, Testimony of James B. Neal, sworn and subscribed before John H. Easton, Justice of the Peace and Coroner.

27. "Verdict of the Coroner's Jury" published in the *Tombstone Daily Epitaph*, Tuesday, July 16,1889.

28. *Tombstone Daily Prospector*, Monday, July 15, 1889. As yet, researchers, including the authors of this book, have not been able to find anyone who would match the person in Galveston, known only as "Kennedy," who was supposedly Buckskin Frank's father. Nor has anything turned up regarding "Thomas Kennedy," the supposed "uncle residing in Houston who is very wealthy, and owns much property there."

29. *Tombstone Daily Epitaph*, Tuesday, July 16, 1889.

30. Ibid., Sunday, September 1, 1889.

31. *Tombstone Daily Epitaph*, Sunday, October 13, 1889.

32. *San Francisco Chronicle*, Saturday, November 30, 1889.

33. *Tombstone Prospector*, Tuesday, December 3,1889.

34. *Santa Cruz Sentinel* (California), Thursday, December 12, 1889. Milton E. Joyce's $30,000 estate in 1889 dollars when converted to 2017 dollars would be the equivalent of $790,000.

35. *Tombstone Prospector*, Friday, December 27, 1889.

36. Ibid., Saturday, December 28, 1889. William C. Staehle had just moved to Tombstone from Phoenix. He was thirty-nine-years-old and was a naturalized citizen who had been born in Germany.

37. *Territory of Arizona v Frank Leslie*, "Affidavit for Postponement of Trial," January 2, 1890, Cochise County District Court, First Judicial District.

38. *Tombstone Prospector*, Friday, January 3, 1890.

39. *Sacramento Daily Record-Union*, Tuesday, January 7, 1890.

Endnotes to Chapter Eleven

1. *Arizona Sentinel* (Yuma), Saturday, January 11, 1890.

2. *Arizona Daily Star* (Tucson), Friday, January 17, 1890, reprinting an item from an earlier date, which had appeared in the *Tombstone Prospector*.

3. *Tombstone Weekly Epitaph*, Saturday, January 18, 1890.

4. *Los Angeles Times*, Tuesday, January 14, 1890.

5. Warden Lon E. Walters Jr. to Robert R. Dykstra January 8, 1953, as cited in Chaput, *"Buckskin Frank" Leslie*, 94 and 131.

6. *Santa Fe New Mexican*, Tuesday, January 14, 1890.

7. *Arizona Daily Citizen* (Tucson), Monday, March 31, 1890.

8. *Tombstone Prospector*, Friday, July 25, 1890.

9. Ibid., Tuesday, September 9, 1890.

10. Ibid., Saturday, December 6, 1890.

11. *San Francisco Chronicle*, Saturday, November 21, 1891.

12. Ibid., Saturday, December 5, 1891.

13. Ibid., Sunday, February 7, 1892.

14. *San Francisco Call*, Tuesday, May 17, 1892.

15. Ibid., May 26, 1892.

16. *San Francisco Chronicle*, Saturday, December 2, 1893.

17. Ibid., Tuesday, March 27, 1894.

18. *Arizona Sentinel* (Yuma), Sunday, April 7, 1894.

19. *Tombstone Weekly Epitaph*, Sunday, June 17, 1894.

20. *Arizona Weekly Citizen* (Tucson), Saturday, January 19, 1895.

21. *Tombstone Weekly Epitaph*, Sunday, December 8, 1895.

22. *Tombstone Prospector*, Monday, June 29, 1896.

23. Proclamation of Pardon, November 17, 1896, Gov. Benjamin J. Franklin Papers, Arizona Department of Archives.

24. Gov. Benjamin J. Franklin to Dr. George Goodfellow, November 18, 1896, Gov. Benjamin J. Franklin Papers, Arizona Department of Archives.

Endnotes to Chapter Twelve

1. Leslie once again spelled his middle name as "Franklyn," rather than "Franklin," on the marriage license. (See chapter one endnote 1.) He also reported his false claim of a Virginia birth on the form, as he had in the *San Francisco Chronicle* of December 2, 1893. Most likely he repeated it on the license for the benefit of his bride, who first became aware of Leslie because of that *Chronicle* article, and may have found a Virginia birth part of his appeal.

2. *Stockton Daily Independent*, Wednesday, December 2, 1896.

3. *San Francisco Call*, Wednesday, April 28, 1897.

Endnotes to Chapter Thirteen

1. *Fort Worth Morning Register*, Thursday, April 8, 1897.

2. Ibid., Wednesday, July 14, 1897. Leslie's friend Libb Wallace had killed a man named Cal Cox in a gunfight at a ranch near Tombstone on February 4, 1889. The following day the *Tombstone Prospector* reported that "Wallace has wealthy and highly respectable parents residing in

Uvalde County, Texas and he is said to be quarrelsome when under the influence of liquor."

3. *Tombstone Prospector*, Monday, September 27, 1897.

4. *Dallas Morning News*, Tuesday, January 18, 1898.

5. *Florence Tribune* (Florence, Arizona), April 2, 1898, reprinting an item that had appeared in *The Oasis* of Nogales, Arizona.

6. "Personal Experiences With the Late General Lawton, Told by Capt. N. Frank Leslie," *San Francisco Call*, Sunday, January 7, 1900. The full text of Leslie's article is given in Appendix C.

7. *Arizona Republican* (Phoenix, Arizona) August 10, 1898, reprinting an item that had appeared in the *Tombstone Prospector*.

8. *The Border Vidette* (Nogales, Arizona), Thursday, December 1, 1898. Edwin T. Dumble (1852-1927) served as Texas State geologist from 1887 to 1897. He was responsible for directing the third Texas Geological Survey, which began in 1889.

9. *The Oasis* (Nogales, Arizona), Saturday, September 2, 1899.

10. Ibid., Saturday, December 16, 1899.

11. *San Francisco Call*, Sunday, January 7, 1900. Major General Henry W. Lawton was born on March 17, 1843, just one day shy of a year after Leslie's March 18, 1842, birth. In 1886 he was selected to lead the expedition that captured Geronimo. During the Spanish-American War he commanded 6,000 troops and fought at the Battle of Las Guasimas and the Siege of Santiago. Once Santiago fell, Lawton served as military governor between August and October 1898. Lawton was killed in the Philippines on December 19, 1899, during the Battle of Paye. He was killed by a sharpshooter under the command of General Licerio Geronimo. The city of Lawton, Oklahoma, founded in 1901, was named in his honor.

12. *The Oasis* (Nogales, Arizona), January 6, 1900.

13. *San Francisco Call*, Saturday, November 3, 1900.

14. *The Oasis* (Nogales, Arizona), Saturday, January 19, 1901.

15. Ibid., Saturday, March 15, 1902.

16. *Louisville Courier-Journal* (Kentucky), Sunday, October 5, 1902.

ENDNOTES TO CHAPTER FOURTEEN

1. *San Francisco Chronicle*, Wednesday, November 26, 1902. Dr. Gustavos A. Weyer, who treated Leslie, was listed as an "Asst Surgeon, Emergency Hospital, 6 Eddy St." in the 1901 San Francisco City Directory. The *San Francisco Call* of November 26, 1902, printed a similar account but gave the correct location of the saloon as being at "Eddy and Market streets," rather than the incorrect "Market and Eddy streets," reported by the *Chronicle*. The *Call* account also stated that "the bullet passed so close to the head that it clipped off a portion of his right ear and cut a furrow along his scalp."

2. *Idaho Falls Times*, Thursday, January 8, 1903. There is no known reason explaining the 43-day time lapse between the *San Francisco Chronicle* account of November 26, 1902, and the *Idaho Falls Times* account of January 8, 1903. While the two accounts describe the same incident, each contains information that the other doesn't. The San Francisco newspaper also describes Leslie's weapon as an automatic pistol, while the Idaho account claimed it was a "revolver."

3. *San Francisco Chronicle*, Friday, April 6, 1906.

4. *Arizona Daily Star* (Tucson), Friday, March 1, 1907.

5. *Houston Post*, Tuesday, March 3, 1908.

6. *Bisbee Daily Review*, Tuesday, June 16, 1908.

7. *San Diego Union*, Sunday, July 26, 1908.

8. 1910 U.S. Federal Census for Berkeley, Alameda County, California.

Endnotes to Chapter Fifteen

1. *Wenatchee Daily World* (Wenatchee, Washington), Monday, May 18, 1908.

2. California State Board of Health, Bureau of Vital Statistics. Certificate of Marriage No. 14014938–Nashville F. Leslie to Elnora Cast, November 6, 1913.

3. *Omak Chronicle* (Omak, Washington), Friday, March 6, 1914.

4. *San Francisco Chronicle*, Saturday, June 5, 1915.

5. *Seattle Daily Times*, Sunday, May 21, 1916. The quote from Leslie provides a rare opportunity to hear him speak in his own words, and understand why he was often described as an "educated" man. The Carranzistas, mentioned by Leslie, were Mexican Revolutionary followers of Venustiano Carranza during 1913 and 1914, who then became the government army until Carranza's overthrow in 1920.

6. *Tombstone Weekly Epitaph*, Sunday, October 14, 1917.

7. The 1920 U.S. Census for Sausalito, Marin County, California. On this census record Leslie once again affirmed he was born in Texas, while he gave his father's birthplace as Virginia and his mother's birthplace as Kentucky. It is significant that the parental birthplace locations of Virginia and Kentucky were identical to what Leslie wrote on his November 6, 1911, Certificate of Marriage to Nora Cast.

8. *Arizona Republican* (Phoenix), Wednesday, April 13, 1921.

9. The Union Leagues were a group of men's clubs established during the Civil War to promote loyalty to the Union, as well as Republican Party values. There were Union League Clubs in several large cities including Philadelphia and San Francisco.

10. Francis Joseph Heney was born in Lima, New York, on March 17, 1859. His family moved to San Francisco when he was four years old. He

studied law in San Francisco and became a member of the bar in 1883. Health problems caused Heney to move to Arizona in 1884, where he ran a cattle business with his brother. He later moved to Tucson where he shot and killed John Handy on September 24, 1891. A court determined that Heney acted in self-defense and he was exonerated. Heney went on to serve as Attorney General of the Arizona Territory from 1893 to 1895. He then moved to San Francisco where he prosecuted Eugene Schmitz and political boss Abraham Ruef for bribery. During the 1907 trial Heney was shot in the head by a juror named Morris Haas, who thought Heney was trying to humiliate him. Heney managed to survive his wound. He died in Santa Monica, California on October 31, 1937.

11. *Tombstone Weekly Epitaph*, Sunday, October 1, 1922.

12. Lt. Col. John R. Dean to William S. Hart, September 9, 1923, William S. Hart Papers, Seaver Center, Natural History Museum, Los Angeles. At the time of Dean's letter, Hart was in the final stages of filming *Wild Bill Hickok*.

13. Supporting players in William S. Hart's *Wild Bill Hickok* included Jack Gardner (1876-1929) who was cast as Bat Masterson and Bert Lindley (1873-1953) who was cast as Wyatt Earp. *Wild Bill Hickok* opened in theatres on November 18, 1923.

ENDNOTES TO CHAPTER SIXTEEN

1. *Santa Cruz Evening News* (California), December 3, 1926.

2. *Los Angeles Times*, Tuesday, December 7, 1926.

3. *Oakland Tribune* (California), Thursday, March 11, 1927.

4. Philip J. Rasch, "A Note on Buckskin Frank Leslie," 19-20.

5. "Leslie, April 1, Frank Leslie age 56 years. Remains at Edwards Brothers. 936 West Sixteenth street." *Los Angeles Times*, Tuesday, April 1, 1924.

6. "Leslie, in this city. Frank Leslie. Remains at Edwards Brothers. 936 West Sixteenth Street." *Los Angeles Times*, April 8, 1924.

7. "Leslie. Services for Frank Leslie will be held today at 2:30 p.m. at the grave in Hollywood Cemetery, under the direction of the Ruppe Mortuary, 842 South Figueroa." *Los Angeles Times*, June 26, 1924.

8. Don Chaput, *"Buckskin Frank" Leslie* (1999), 114.

9. Robert Mullin to Stuart N. Lake, August 22, 1953. Rasch Collection, Arizona Historical Society.

10. *San Bernardino Daily Sun* (California) Wednesday, September 9, 1925.

11. *The Morning Oregonian* (Portland), Saturday, October 16, 1926.

12. Tom Bailey, "I Saw Wyatt Earp's Commission," *True West*, January-February 1961, 54-55.

13. *Healdsburg Tribune* (California), Wednesday, November 2, 1927.

14. The San Francisco Bay Area, usually called simply The Bay Area, consists of nine counties: Alameda, Contra Costa, Marin, Napa, San Francisco, San Mateo, Santa Clara, Solano, and Sonoma. The Bay Area also includes cities where Leslie's residence has been documented, such as San Francisco, Berkeley, and Sausalito.

15. *San Francisco Chronicle*, Wednesday, November 2, 1927.

16. *Bellingham Herald* (Washington), Thursday, November 3, 1927.

17. Edward O. Heinrich was born in Wisconsin in 1881. He arrived at the Berkeley campus of the University of California's College of Chemistry with only $18 in his pocket, worked his way through and graduated in 1908 with a degree in chemical engineering. Heinrich went on to become chief of police at Alameda, California, and saw to it that his police force was trained in the latest advancements in scientific crime scene investigation. He moved to San Francisco in 1919 and lectured on

criminal investigation at the University of California at Berkeley. Before he died in 1953, Heinrich saw police departments across the county adopt many of his innovations.

18. *Oakland Tribune* (California), Sunday, November 6, 1927.

19. Ibid., Wednesday, November 9,1927.

20. *San Francisco Chronicle*, Thursday, December 29, 1927.

21. By the time the U.S. Census was taken for Omak, Washington, Leslie's last wife, who gave her name as "Elnora Leslie," described herself as being "widowed." This indicates that she may have somehow learned of Leslie's death in El Cerrito, California, during October 1927.

Selected Bibliography

Books

Bailey, Lynn R. *Tombstone: "Too Tough to Die," The Rise, Fall and Resurrection of a Silver Mining Camp—1878 to 1990.* Tucson: Westernlore Press, 2004.

Ball, Larry D. *Tom Horn: In Life and Legend.* Norman: University of Oklahoma Press, 2014.

Bourke, John G. *An Apache Campaign in the Sierra Madre.* New York: Charles Scribner's Sons, 1886.

———. *On the Border With Crook.* New York: Charles Scribner's Sons, 1891.

Breakenridge, William M. *Helldorado: Bringing the Law to the Mesquite.* Boston and New York: Houghton Mifflin Company, 1928.

Burns, Walter Noble. *Tombstone: An Iliad of the Southwest.* Garden City, NY: Doubleday, Page & Company, 1927.

Carmony, Neil B., ed. *Tombstone's Violent Years, 1880–1882, As Remembered by John Plesent Gray.* Tucson, AZ: Trail to Yesterday Books, 1999.

Chaput, Don. *"Buckskin Frank" Leslie.* Tucson, AZ: Westernlore Press, 1999.

Dempsey, David, and Raymond P. Baldwin. *The Triumphs and Trials of Lotta Crabtree.* New York: William Morrow & Company, Inc., 1968.

Dodge, Fred. *Under Cover for Wells Fargo: The Unvarnished Recollections of Fred Dodge.* edited by Carolyn Lake. Boston: Houghton Mifflin Company, 1969.

Dworkin, Mark J. *American Mythmaker: Walter Noble Burns and the Legends of Billy the Kid, Wyatt Earp and Joaquin Murrieta.* Norman: University of Oklahoma Press, 2015.

Erwin, Allen A. *The Southwest of John Horton Slaughter.* Glendale, CA: The Arthur H. Clark Company, 1965.

Faulk, Odie B. *The Geronimo Campaign.* New York: Oxford University Press, 1969.

———. *Tombstone: Myth and Reality.* New York: Oxford University Press, 1972.

Horn, Tom. *Life of Tom Horn: Government Scout and Interpreter Written by Himself, Together with His Letters and Statements by His Friends. A Vindication.* Denver, CO: The Louthan Book Company, 1904.

Hutton, Paul Andrew. *The Apache Wars: The Hunt for Geronimo, the Apache Kid, and the Captive Boy Who Started the Longest War in American History.* New York: Crown Publishing Group, 2016.

Lummis, Charles Fletcher. *General Crook and the Apache Wars.* Flagstaff, AZ: Northland Press, 1966.

Marks, Paula Mitchell. *And Die in the West: The Story of the O.K. Corral Gunfight.* New York: William Morrow and Company, Inc., 1989.

Martin, Douglas D. *Tombstone's Epitaph.* Albuquerque: The University of New Mexico Press, 1951.

Martin, Douglas D. *Silver, Sex and Six Guns: Tombstone Saga of Buckskin Frank Leslie.* Tombstone, AZ: Published by the Tombstone Epitaph, 1962.

Myers, John Myers. *The Last Chance: Tombstone's Early Years.* New York: E.P. Dutton & Co., Inc., 1950.

Parsons, George Whitwell. *The Private Journal of George W. Parsons.* Tombstone, AZ: Published by the Tombstone Epitaph, 1972.

———. *A Tenderfoot in Tombstone. The Private Journal of George Whitwell Parsons: The Turbulent Years, 1880-82.* Tucson, AZ: Westernlore Press, 1996.

———. *The Devil Has Foreclosed: The Private Journal of George Whitwell Parsons: The Concluding Arizona Years, 1882-87.* Tucson, AZ: Westernlore Press, 1997.

Rickards, Colin. *Buckskin Frank Leslie: Gunman of Tombstone.* El Paso, TX: Texas Western Press, 1964.

Roberts, Gary L. *Doc Holliday: The Life and Legend.* Hoboken, NJ: John Wiley & Sons, Inc., 2006.

Rose, John D. *"Buckskin Frank" Leslie's Deadly Tombstone Love Triangle.* Sierra Vista, AZ: John Rose Historical Publications, 2016.

Shillingberg, William B. *Tombstone, A. T.: A History of Early Mining, Milling, and Mayhem.* Spokane, WA: The Arthur H. Clark Company, 1999.

Smith, Grant H., and Joseph V. Tingley. *The History of the Comstock Lode 1850-1997.* Reno: University of Nevada Press, 1998.

Sonnichsen, Charles Leland. *Billy King's Tombstone.* Caldwell, ID: The Caxton Printers, Ltd., 1942.

Sweeney, Edwin R. *From Cochise to Geronimo: The Chiricahua Apaches, 1874-1886.* Norman: The University of Oklahoma Press, 2012.

Tefertiller, Casey. *Wyatt Earp: The Life Behind the Legend.* New York: John Wiley & Sons, Inc., 1997.

Thrapp, Dan L. *Al Sieber: Chief of Scouts.* Norman: University of Oklahoma Press, 1964.

———. *The Conquest of Apacheria.* Norman: University of Oklahoma Press, 1967.

Traywick, Ben T. *Tombstone's "Buckskin Frank": Nashville Franklyn Leslie.* Tombstone, AZ: Published by Red Marie's, 2013.

Turner, Alford E., ed. *The Earps Talk.* College Station, TX: Creative Publishing Company, 1980.

Walters, Lorenzo D. *Tombstone's Yesterday.* Tucson, AZ: Acme Printing Co., 1928.

Articles

Bailey, Tom. "I Saw Wyatt Earp's Commission." *True West,* January-February, 1961.

DeMattos, Jack. "Gunfighters of the Real West: Buckskin Frank Leslie." *Real West*, September 1981.

———. "Buckskin Frank Leslie Revealed." *Wild West History Association Journal* 8, no. 3 (June 2015).

———. "Buckskin Frank Leslie." *True West*, November 2016.

Leslie, Nashville Franklyn. "Personal Experiences With the Late General Lawton Told By Captain N. Frank Leslie, His Chief of Scouts in the Apache Campaign." *San Francisco Call*, Sunday, January 7, 1900.

O'Neal, Bill. "Buckskin Frank Leslie vs Billy the Kid Claiborne." *True West*, March 1991.

Parker, Lowell. "Ladykiller Leslie Also Mankiller." (First of Three Parts) *Arizona Republic* (Phoenix), Monday, August 15, 1977.

———. "Woman Trouble Began Leslie's Decline." (Second of Three Parts) *Arizona Republic* (Phoenix) Tuesday, August 16, 1977.

———. "For Once, Leslie Missed His Shot." (Third of Three Parts) *Arizona Republic* (Phoenix), Wednesday, August 17, 1977.

Rasch, Philip J. "A Note on Buckskin Frank Leslie." Denver Westerners *Brand Book* 10 (1954).

Scott, Jay. "Buckskin Frank: Tombstone Lady Killer." *True Western Adventures*, April 1961.

NEWSPAPERS

Arizona Daily Citizen (Tucson)—March 31, 1890.

Arizona Daily Star (Tucson)—September 29, 1880; October 30, 1880; February 18, 1883; February 22, 1883; February 27, 1883; April 3, 1883; April 19, 1883; June 3, 1883; March 1, 1884; August 1, 1885; August 18 , 1885; January 17, 1890; and March 1, 1907.

Arizona Republican (Phoenix)—August 10, 1898, and April 13, 1921.

Arizona Sentinel (Yuma)—January 11, 1890, and April 7, 1894.

Arizona Weekly Citizen (Tucson)—October 2, 1880; March 27, 1881; August 28, 1881; December 24, 1882; April 21, 1883; May 5, 1883; May

19, 1883; October 20, 1883; June 20, 1885; August 22, 1885; July 20, 1889, and January 19, 1895.

Bellingham Herald (Washington)—November 3, 1927.

Bisbee Daily Review (Arizona) —June 16, 1908, and March 27, 1934.

Daily Alta California (San Francisco) —June 11, 1869.

Daily Tombstone—July 31, 1885; October 27, 1885; May 13, 1886; and May 17, 1886.

Dallas Morning News —January 18, 1898.

Florence Tribune (Florence, Arizona) —April 2, 1898.

Fort Worth Morning Register —April 8, 1897, and June 14, 1897.

Healdsburg Tribune (California) —November 2, 1927.

Houston Post —March 3, 1908.

Idaho Falls Times — January 8, 1903.

Los Angeles Daily Herald —March 28, 1883, and March 5, 1889.

Los Angeles Times—November 9, 1882; April 17, 1886; April 1, 1924; April 8, 1924; June 26, 1924; and December 7, 1926.

Oakland Tribune (California) —March 31, 1927.

Omak Chronicle (Omak, Washington) —March 6, 1914.

Sacramento Daily Record-Union —March 15, 1883; August 7, 1883; and January 7, 1890.

San Bernardino Daily Sun (California) —September 9, 1927.

San Diego Union — July 26, 1908.

San Francisco Call —April 28, 1897; January 7, 1900; and November 3, 1900.

San Francisco Chronicle —Sunday, April 4, 1886; November 30, 1889; November 21, 1891; December 5, 1891; February 7, 1892; December 2, 1893; November 26, 1902; April 6, 1906; June 5, 1915; and December 29, 1927.

San Jose Evening News (California) —Thursday, March 11, 1886.

Santa Cruz Evening News (California) — Friday, December 3, 1926.

Santa Cruz Sentinel (California) —July 12, 1885; May 10, 1887; and December 12, 1889.

Santa Fe Daily New Mexican —April 20, 1883, and January 14, 1890.

Seattle Daily Times (Washington) —May 21, 1916.

Sierra County Advocate (Hillsborough, New Mexico) —May 28, 1889.

St. Johns Herald (Arizona) —July 15, 1886.

Stockton Daily Independent (California) —December 2, 1896.

The Border Vidette (Nogales, Arizona) —December 1, 1898.

The Morning Oregonian — October 16, 1926.

The Oasis (Nogales, Arizona) —September 2, 1899; December 16, 1899; January 6, 1900; January 19, 1901; and March 15, 1902.

Tombstone Daily Epitaph —July 22, 1880; August 24, 1880; August 25, 1880; September 23, 1880; October 27, 1880; December 14, 1880; November 13, 1881; December 8, 1881; January 10, 1882; March 16, 1882; May 1, 1882; June 7, 1882; November 18, 1882; January 14, 1886; February 14, 1886; March 10, 1886; March 26, 1886; April 4, 1886; May 18, 1886; June 10, 1886; September 11, 1886; February 11, 1887; March 9, 1887; March 22, 1887; June 16, 1887; July 12, 1889; July 16, 1889; August 28, 1889; September 1, 1889; and October 13, 1889.

Tombstone Democrat —Wednesday, March 9, 1887.

Tombstone Nugget —August 20, 1881 and May 1, 1882.

Tombstone Prospector —January 21, 1889; February 5, 1889; April 6, 1889; July 15, 1889; December 3, 1889; December 27, 1889; December 28, 1890; January 3, 1890; July 25, 1890; September 9, 1890; June 29, 1896; and September 27, 1897.

Tombstone Weekly Epitaph —December 19, 1881; April 10, 1882; September 23, 1882; October 28, 1882; November 11, 1882; April 25, 1886; June 12, 1887; July 17, 1887; September 10, 1887; January 18, 1890; June 17, 1894; and October 1, 1922.

Tombstone Weekly Prospector —Sunday, October 23, 1887.

Truckee Tribune (California)—Saturday, March 13, 1869.

Weekly Arizona Miner (Prescott, Arizona) —Friday, December 23, 1881.

Weekly Phoenix Herald (Arizona) —Thursday, November 8, 1883.

Wenatchee Daily World (Washington)—Monday, May 18, 1908.

Arizona Voter Registrations, 1866-1955

July 13, 1880 (# 2503) —Nashville F. Leslie, age 36 [*sic*], Pima County, Arizona. (Pima County, Arizona, was sub-divided and Cochise County, Arizona, was created on February 1, 1881, out of the eastern portion of Pima County, where Tombstone was located).

December 5, 1881 (# 810) —Nashville Franklin [*sic*] Leslie, age 39, U.S. Scout, Cochise County, Arizona.

August 24, 1882 (# 1057) —Nashville F. Leslie, age 40, Saloon Keeper, Cochise County, Arizona.

August 23, 1886 (# 1204) —Nashville Franklin [*sic*] Leslie, age 44, Rancher, Cochise County, Arizona."

August 24, 1888 (# 997) —Nashville F. Leslie, age 46, Rancher, Cochise County, Arizona.

Census Records

1880 United States Federal Census for Tombstone Village, Pima County, Arizona: "Leslie, Frank, age 35 [*sic*], Saloon Keeper, born Texas."

1910 United States Federal Census for Berkeley, Alameda County, California: "Leslie, Frank, age 65 [*sic*], Servant, born Texas."

1920 United States Federal Census for Sausalito, Marin County, California: "Leslie, Nashville F., age 77, Lodger, Single, born Texas."

City Directory Records

1878 *San Francisco City Directory* (515) —"Leslie, Frank – 732 Howard Street."

1879 *San Francisco City Directory* (527) – "Leslie, Frank – 90 Third Street."

1880 *San Francisco City Directory* (546) –"Leslie, Frank – 746 Folsom Street."

1905 *San Francisco City Directory* (1,124) –"Leslie, Nashville F., 122 7th."

1908 *Oakland, California City Directory* (1,352) ––"Leslie, Frank N. [*sic*], miner, 1348 Shattuck Avenue, Berkeley."

1909 *Oakland, California City Directory* (1,106) –"Leslie, N. Frank, mining, 1348 Shattuck Avenue, Berkeley."

1911 *Oakland, California City Directory* (1,108) –"Leslie, N. Frank, 2918 Ellsworth, Berkeley."

Marriage and Divorce Records

April 13, 1880 (Tombstone, Arizona) – Mary Jane Evans married Michael D. Killeen. Louisa Bilicke was the Maid of Honor. Nashville Franklyn Leslie was the Best Man.

July 6, 1880 (Tombstone, Arizona) – Mary Jane Evans Killeen married Nashville Franklyn Leslie. Justice James Reilly performed the ceremony. Louisa Bilicke was the Maid of Honor. Col. F. Hines was the Best Man. (*Docket "A," 159, Precinct 17, Pima County, Arizona. Records of the Justice's Court of James Reilly*, Cochise County Recorder's Office, Bisbee, Arizona.)

June 3, 1887 (Tombstone, Arizona) –Mary Jane Evans Killeen Leslie was granted a divorce from Nashville Franklyn Leslie by Judge William H. Barnes.

December 1, 1896 (Stockton, California) –Belle Stowell married Nashville Franklyn Leslie. The ceremony was performed by Justice Parker.

March 19, 1903 (San Francisco, California) –The *San Francisco Call* reported that a divorce was granted to "Belle Leslie from N.F. Leslie for failure to provide."

November 6, 1913 (Napa, California) –Elnora Torbert Cast married Nashville Franklyn Leslie. They were married by a Justice of the

Peace. (California State Board of Health, Bureau of Vital Statistics. *Certificate of Marriage No. 14014938 —Nashville F. Leslie to Elnora Cast, Nov. 6, 1913.*)

Index